JASON VALE

A little sprinkle of inspiration

First published in 2018 by Create Magic Publications

2

ISBN: 978-1-9993102-0-2

www.createmagicpublications.com

This book is dedicated to

Little JJ

My Boy – My World – My Magic

....

His amazing mother

Katie

My Girl – My World – My Magic

....

My beautiful god-daughter

Robyn

....

...and to ***all*** the wonderful
Magic Makers in the world

MAGICAL CONTENTS

BE
A
MAGIC
MAKER

1

We all need a sprinkle of magic in our lives every now and then, but what many don't realise is the best way to experience magic throughout your life is to create it at every opportunity.

If you want to experience more love, *create magic*. If you want to smile more, *create magic*. If you want better relationships, *create magic*. If you want a business that truly thrives, *create magic*. If you want purpose, *create magic*. If you want to feel truly alive, *create magic*. If you want more fun, *create magic*. In short, if you want to feel magic in every area of your life, all you have to do is create it!

Hello, I'm Jason Vale and thank you for taking the time to read this book. The subheading was going to be 'The Little Book with a Huge Impact', because if used correctly that's precisely what it has the power to do. Once you fully understand how creating magic for yourself and others has an automatic positive effect on every aspect of your own life, you won't be able to resist becoming a magic maker for as many people as you can, as often as you can.

Just so you know where I'm coming from: this isn't 'the Universe will provide if you just ask' hippy stuff, because that's not how life works! This book is full of logical, practical and genuinely effective advice that will come into play every single time it's put into practice. And that's the difference; you must go *beyond* simply asking the Universe to provide and meet it at least half way. If you want to build muscle, you cannot manifest it by simply staring at weights in the gym, and asking the Universe to provide you with the body of your dreams – you need to act. I appreciate there is power in what people call 'the law of attraction' and the idea of what you put out there you get back tenfold. But you do actually need to put something out there other than just mantras. The Universe will not provide something for you unless you provide something for the Universe! The difference between the '*create magic*' philosophy and 'the law of attraction' is that the philosophy of creating magic works every single time you apply it. This is a bold statement, I know, but you simply cannot create magic for others without automatically creating magic for yourself.

This little book will take less than an afternoon to read, but don't be mistaken in thinking something this small can't have a massive impact on you and those around you. It was the late Dame

Anita Roddick (founder of The Body Shop) who famously said:

> *'If you think you're too small to have an impact, try going to bed with a mosquito.'*

And that's the aim of this little book, to have a huge and profound impact on as many people around the world as possible. That's why ten per cent of all profits will go directly into a *Create Magic Fund*, set up to do just that: create magic for as many people as possible. Just by buying this book you have already helped to create magic for others, even if you didn't know it.

I'm hoping this book will create an army, or family, of magic makers across the world; people who ask themselves '*the magic question*' whenever and wherever possible. People who understand just how powerful this question can be when asked with genuine conviction. People who instantly smile and get excited the second they ask this question. People who understand the genuine difference this question can make to their lives and the lives of others. An army of magic makers all over the world, waking up asking themselves the magic question and creating magic as they go. The question – although deceptively simple – has the potential to have a bigger positive impact on your life, and the lives of others, than any other question you could consistently ask yourself. And what is the magic question I hear you ask?

'HOW CAN I CREATE MAGIC FOR...?'

It's up to you how you choose to finish the question, but the seed of magic is planted the very second you ask it. When you ask yourself, 'How can I create magic for a certain individual, a group of people, a total stranger or myself?' with *genuine* conviction, and you allow time for your brain to search for answers, you cannot help but come up with a plethora of wonderful options. That's the beauty of the magic question; the options your brain provides will always be wonderful because you are about to create magic for yourself, someone else, or both.

When you start to tap into the power of becoming a magic maker, every single area of your life instantly becomes more magical as a result. It doesn't matter if you're asking the question in your relationship, your work, your business, your personal life or any area of your life for that matter; it becomes more exciting, uplifting, rewarding, fulfilling, successful and, of course, magical. I will give several examples throughout this little book, and I'm hoping that when you see the sort of positive impact asking *the Question* can have, you'll instantly want to join the magic-making army and start creating magic for yourself, those around you, and even complete strangers, as soon as you can.

THE MAGIC OF REPETITION

Although the message of this book is simplistic, there are some key fundamentals of magic making that need to be adhered to in order to maximise your magic-making potential. To make sure these don't get glossed over or missed, I will be repeating certain points throughout the book to make sure they are firmly locked in. So, if you read something and think you've read a similar point earlier in the book, chances are you have – it's intentional!

THE MAGIC OF AN OPEN MIND

I'd also like to add, that to get the most out of this book, you need to read it with an open mind. I am perhaps one of the most dismissive and sceptical people I know. I tend to judge things quite early on, or shut something down before I've finished it if there's something I don't agree with. I would encourage you – even if something jars slightly – including my style of writing (it's not for everyone!) – to move past it with an open mind in order to take in the message. By the time you come to the end of the book, all bases will have been covered, and all – hopefully – will make sense. This book has also been written in a specific order, so please don't skip through the pages or read chapters randomly. It has been designed to take you on a magical journey, so that by the time you reach the end, your desire to add a little magic making to your life will be overwhelming.

The first thing you need to understand about being a magic maker is that it's impossible to create magic for others without creating magic for yourself. Which brings me on to the first rule of magic...

THE JOEY RULE

There's No Such Thing As A Selfless Good Deed

2

My favourite US sitcom of all time is F.R.I.E.N.D.S. And even if you haven't seen it, the chances are – given that it's the most successful global sitcom of all time – you'll have heard of it. In one of the episodes, one of the six main characters, Joey Tribbiani, points out that there's no such thing as a selfless good deed. He even challenges Phoebe, one of the other characters, to try and do a truly selfless act. Phoebe fails. Why? Because ultimately there is no such thing as a selfless good deed. You may think you are doing a good deed purely for someone else, but no matter what the good deed is, somewhere along the line it makes *you* feel good too. That's why, and I don't mind repeating this point throughout the book:

YOU CANNOT CREATE MAGIC FOR OTHERS WITHOUT CREATING MAGIC FOR YOURSELF AT THE SAME TIME!

For example, if you pass a homeless person on the street and you give them some money, or nip into a shop and buy them a sandwich and a coffee, this isn't purely selfless, because it makes you feel good too. It may appear on the surface that you're only doing it for the good of that person, but because it inevitably makes you feel good, it's never one hundred per cent selfless. If you help someone struggling to cross the road – same thing – it makes you feel good. If you give money to charity, cook someone dinner, run your partner a candlelit bath, help to carry someone's bags, open the door for someone, give someone a massage, send someone a lovely card or gift, it's never self*less*. Nor, however, is it self*ish*. It's the perfect balance of magic being created across the board, and this is why it's impossible to become a magic maker without experiencing magic yourself. This doesn't mean that when people create magic for others they are *consciously* creating magic for themselves at the same time. The vast majority of magic making is consciously done selflessly; but there is always a secondary gain for the magic makers themselves – even if they aren't aware of it. This is one of the wonderful side effects of becoming a magic maker; you cannot create magic for others without also creating magic for yourself. It's '*the Joey Rule*' – so just know if you do create magic for others, somewhere along the line you'll be getting a benefit too.

THERE'S NO SUCH THING AS A SELFLESS GOOD DEED

Take this book as an example. Why am I writing it? Why am I not on the beach (which is extremely near as I write this), kicking back with a cool drink and enjoying the sun, surf and sea? Why am I choosing to sit in the shade on a beautiful July day in the Algarve in Portugal, rather than doing one of a million other pleasurable things which are available to me today? Because writing this book excites me; it stimulates me; it makes me feel incredible to think this little book has the potential to grow many magical tentacles to help create magic for hundreds or even thousands of people from all over the world. I type away because I feel inspired knowing that some profit from this book will go into a *Create Magic Fund* that will help to create incredible amounts of magic for others. But I'm not doing it selflessly, and that's my point (or rather Joey's). If you create magic for others, you inevitably create some magic for yourself – and therefore there is no such thing as a selfless good deed. The level of magic created for you will vary on the magic scale, but you will always experience *some* magic if you do a good deed for someone else.

I was challenged on this recently after I did a mini talk on the '*create magic*' philosophy. A woman said that she and others had been discussing *the Joey Rule* and that it's flawed as there are genuine examples of totally selfless acts of magic making. The first example she gave was of someone who gave one of their kidneys to a family member who would have otherwise died without it. I explained that on the surface this appears incredibly selfless, but ultimately it never is. Not only would this monumental magical act make the person who is giving the kidney feel heroic on a scale few of us will ever experience, but they would also be helping to save the life of someone they love dearly and, no doubt, whose departure from this world would have caused them enormous long-term pain. Without question, the act of giving a kidney is heroic beyond words and it takes a special kind of person to do something so magical, but it's not *completely* selfless. Even if the person isn't consciously doing it for any reward or gain, inevitably they will also experience some magic because of the magic they created for someone else.

I will litter the book with examples of this, but perhaps one of the most powerful examples that springs to mind came before Mother's Day this year, when I asked myself a truly magical question that has changed this time of year for me in the most positive way. And what was the question? How can I create...

THE MOTHER OF ALL MAGIC

3

Just to give some background before I give this powerful example of *the Joey Rule* – my mum passed away nine years ago. She was my everything. I realise people often say that, but if you ever had the good fortune of meeting this truly incredible woman, you'll know what I am talking about. I grew up in a very rough part of London; we had no money, I'm an only child and I never knew my father. I left school at fifteen because I needed to work when mum couldn't anymore after a botched operation. She had a cyst the size of an orange on one of her ovaries and had surgery to remove it. The trouble was the doctor had a bad day at the office and removed the wrong ovary.

My mum was not only my mother; she was my father, brother, sister, best friend and soul mate. She was also the most prolific magic maker I have ever known. She consistently showed how you could create magic for others wherever you go, regardless of how much money you have in your bank account. If she was down to her last penny and it was between her or someone on the street having that penny, the person on the street would get it every time – no question! The incredible magic my mother created for others no doubt created some magic for her at the same time, which is the beauty of magic making and in keeping with *the Joey Rule*. I could wax lyrical about this wonderful woman for several books, let alone pages, but the reason I bring up her up is because of what happened on Mother's Day this year.

As you can imagine, ever since my mum passed away at the tender age of 63, Mother's Day hasn't been a picnic for me. It's in your face for many weeks before the day itself, and impossible to ignore. Constant TV adverts and social media posts wherever you look means you're constantly bombarded by advertisers telling you how to make your Mother's Day that little bit more special. This has been without question the hardest and saddest thing about every Mother's Day since she died, knowing that no matter how much I want to create magic for her, I no longer can. What makes it harder is I'm now in the financially privileged position where I could create crazy magic for her and fulfil her lifetime dreams; but I can't, and it hurts like hell. The saddest thing about our health retreat in Portugal is knowing that the one mum who will never get to experience this beautiful place is my *own* magic-making mum.

For the last nine years, I have resented Mother's

Day and, if I'm honest, I've resented everyone who has a mum that they can create magic for. I have usually kept myself to myself, and hoped the day would pass as soon as possible. That was until this year.

THE LOWEST PLACE ON EARTH

When my mum died, I went to the Dead Sea in Israel. I felt the lowest I had ever felt in my life and knew my mum, who had the darkest sense of humour of anyone I knew, would appreciate me literally going to the lowest place on Earth, just when I thought I couldn't get any lower. But I soon realised that no matter where you go – including over four hundred meters below sea level – you take yourself with you, making it impossible to run away from that kind of grief.

I found myself going back to the Dead Sea this year, just a week before Mother's Day. On social media the usual adverts started popping up, along with people telling the world what sort of magic they would be creating for their mum this coming Mother's Day. Once again, I felt incredibly resentful, angry and hurt, because I was no longer in a position to create magic for my mum. I started to go into the usual downward spiral, but then I asked myself a different question – a question which means, although Mother's Day will never be a bed of roses for me, it will be a day that I can look forward to and embrace fully from now on.

MAKE MY MOTHER'S DAY

I knew I couldn't create magic for my own mum, so I simply asked myself, 'If I can't create magic for my own mum, can I create some magic for someone else's?' This question was life-changing. Far from dreading the following Mothering Sunday, I got disproportionately excited. I immediately called the office back in the UK, and put a plan in place to create magic for someone else's mum for Mother's Day. My idea was to give a free place at my *Juicy Oasis* Health Retreat in Portugal to a deserving mum, and her son/daughter, through a competition called *Make My Mother's Day*. I asked people to send an email telling me why they thought their mum was deserving of the free place. I had no idea how many people would enter, but was blown away when, within days, thousands of entries began flooding in. Please understand there weren't just thousands of names to choose from – there were also thousands of extremely moving, often long stories of incredible mums who had been through a lot. Mums who desperately needed a break and reminding that they were loved. Mums who had spent their lives creating magic for others, and who now needed to experience some real magic for themselves. I spent hours reading as many as

I could to select one worthy mum to create magic for on Mother's Day. The stories were, as you can imagine, unbelievably moving, and it was incredibly hard to choose. But in the end, I chose this one:

....

> "Hi Jason, I follow your page on insta and me and my mum dream of coming to one of your retreats! I believe my mum should win because she is my absolute angel, and an inspiration and even having had a tough life, remains the most positive person, so I want to send her to your amazing retreat so she leaves a healthier/happier person.
>
> She's a single mother of 3 and has been since we were 7 and has struggled to raise us but (if I do say so myself) has raised three kind/successful children at the sacrifice of her own life/dreams.
>
> When me and my twin brother hit adulthood, and she was free to live her life, she was diagnosed with breast cancer which she battled for months, remaining positive the whole time and still continuing her job at a boarding school and taking part in fundraising

events for Cancer Research and other charities. Shortly after she was diagnosed, so was her partner of 10 years. When she learned she had beat cancer, we already knew it wasn't going to be the case for him, and six months later she lost him, but she deals with her grief/guilt of surviving what he couldn't to remain the ever positive person she is.

She had four good years after that and started travelling more and I felt like she was beginning to enjoy life again when in August last year she was diagnosed with a different kind of breast cancer in her other breast. We are nearly at the end of her treatment now and she remains the same positive crazy person (amongst the expected bad days) and we are hoping for the same results as last time so she can live a life that doesn't revolve around scans/ injections/ chemo etc. Although I have looked into it and it's not something we could afford for a few years I definitely think a retreat, where she can be in the most beautiful surroundings and give her body all the good stuff it needs would be perfect for her! Whether we win this or not we will see you one day, I just hope you agree this superwoman deserves it so it can be sooner. Please don't take this as a sob story because we are all so positive and have each

> other which is enough to keep her happy but Mum is so kind and puts everyone else first even on her toughest days, so I would love to be able to give something as amazing as she is back to her on Mother's Day.
>
> Thanks for taking the time to read this and consider my superstar mum x"

....

I think what resonated with me most was the fact that she was a single parent (like my mum), who had sacrificed her own life dreams (like my mum), had cancer twice (like my mum), lost her partner through cancer (like my mum), and has still remained incredibly strong and positive, no matter what life has thrown at her (like my mum had before she died). However, one thing I have learned over the many years I've been on this planet is that no matter how strong someone appears to be on the surface, they might be struggling more than you'll ever know when their bedroom door shuts. This became very apparent when I made the call. Not only did I want to create magic by giving away the retreat place, but I also wanted to call them personally on Mother's Day to surprise them. When I called, what was even more wonderful was the mum in question didn't know who I was, what I did, or what *Juicy Oasis* was. I told her that her daughter had written to us and wanted to make her day on Mother's Day. She didn't fully understand what was happening, didn't believe it, and sounded a little, well, underwhelmed at first. But when I said the words, 'Your daughter told me what you've been through and it sounds like you need a break', she broke down. Her normal, strong, 'I can deal with anything' attitude came crumbling down, and the tears started to flow – followed by mine!

I haven't told this story to say, 'Hey, look at me and the nice thing I did', because when you account for *the Joey Rule*, that's never the case. There is, after all, no such thing as a selfless good deed, because when you create magic you get magic back; it's once again the beautiful magic of creating magic.

ONE BIT OF MAGIC LEADS TO ANOTHER

Here's how it works. I decided to create magic for a stranger's mum, which in turn created magic for me. Not simply because it made me feel good on a day I never thought I could feel good again, but because I also know if my mum is anywhere watching, then creating magic for others on that day would create magic for her on a level far greater than anything I could have ever bought for her. The daughter, in creating magic for her mum (which she no doubt wanted to do because her mum had clearly created magic for her throughout her life), inevitably got a great deal of magic for herself in return. Not only does she get the instant magic of feeling good because she's done something lovely for her mum, but she also gets to come on the retreat with her! They get a week of pure mother-daughter magic at a magical place. The magic this one event created doesn't stop there either – as I'll explain much more in *The Ripple Of Magic* chapter later. You need to realise that when you create magic, it leads to more magic, and once the snowball has started there's little you can do to stop it. Every Mother's Day will no longer be tinged with the same level of sadness, because every Mother's Day I now get the opportunity to create magic for someone else's mum.

Once you start asking yourself *the* question and begin to fully understand *the Joey Rule*, pure magic is yours for the taking. You will also be able to tap into more magic, more often, when you realise magic isn't always grown on...

THE MAGIC MONEY TREE

4

You don't need to have money to create magic. In fact, often it's the little moments of magic created with pure imagination and forethought – rather than money – that are often the ones that create the biggest magic moments of all. Don't get me wrong, if you happen to have money, there's clearly a different kind of magic that can be created. For example, my mum always wanted a nice home and an old 1960s convertible Mercedes. If she were alive today, I am lucky enough to be in a position where I could give these to her in a heartbeat. These two things, without question, would have created magic for her. However, I know they would pale into insignificance compared to when I made her breakfast in bed for the first time as a kid, or when I drew her a picture, or made her a ceramic apple in primary school. Although the breakfast was no doubt horrendous, the picture certainly not worthy of the Tate Gallery, and the ceramic apple the worst thing ever made in any pottery class ever (it was horrific!), to my mum I know these things created magic way beyond anything money could buy. Oh, and the reason I know why? Even though the ceramic apple was the most god-awful piece of pottery, she kept it out, on display, for the world to see. It was no doubt as ugly as hell to anyone else, including me – but to her it was pure magic. I cannot wait for the first morning our little JJ (who is just six months old at the time of writing this book) makes us breakfast in bed – I already know it will be the most magical breakfast we will ever have the privilege of eating.

THE BEST NATION ON EARTH!

Some of the finest magical moments I have ever experienced, whether it's me trying to create magic for someone else, creating it purely for myself or someone creating magic for me, have required little or no money. The point is that you don't have to pick from the '*magic money tree*' in order to create magic. You can, but there are a million different ways true magic can also be created without money. *You* are the magic maker and the only thing standing between you and creating magic is your mind.

One of my favourite Christmas films of all time is *Miracle On 34th Street* (*It's A Wonderful Life* is obviously my all-time fave!) and one of the loveliest lines in the film is, 'The best nation in the world is not the English nation or the German nation or the American nation… but the Imagi*nation*', and, as corny as that line is, never a truer line was uttered. That's why it's important when you ask yourself the question, 'How can I create magic for...?', you allow your brain time to truly tap into the best nation on earth. There may not be an instant answer, or the first answer may not be the best, but if you allow your imagination time, different ways of how *you* can create magic in *your* own personal circumstances, with the resources *you* personally have at your disposal, ideas will start flowing. For some, magic making may well involve spending a lot of money, for others a little, and for some none at all. But ultimately, the only thing that can ever really prevent you from creating magic is a lack of imagination, not a lack of money. However, if you have money and wish to create magic with it, that can be pretty cool too.

THE MAGIC OF BUDDHA

One of the most magical and long lasting moments I ever created for my mum did in fact involve money. She loved Buddha; the house had quite a few of them littered around the place and, although not religious at all, she just liked and felt a spiritual connection to him.

We were walking past a shop when I was 13 years old and in the window was the most magnificent Buddha. It was big – much bigger than any she owned. She looked at the price; it was £16.

Now this won't seem like a great deal of money to many, but firstly, it was 1982 (when £16 was *very* different to £16 today) and secondly, we really didn't have any money. Although I knew there was no way of getting her dream Buddha there and then, I knew I would find a way. I went back to the shop and asked if I could give the owner a £1 deposit and pay £1 for the next 15 weeks. I explained this was my mum's dream Buddha, but she couldn't afford it. It was the only one in the shop and I was scared it would have sold before I could save up in time. I was working a Saturday job that paid £8 a day, so I knew I could spare £1 of it. The shop owner agreed and 16 weeks later I walked out of the shop with the Buddha. To say it was hard to carry home on the bus was an understatement, but the magical Buddha made it. I say magical Buddha, not because I'm a spiritual person myself and believe there is any actual magic in Buddha per se, but because of the degree of magic it created for my mum and for me.

I had the good fortune of seeing my mum smile on many occasions throughout her life and I have also seen her truly moved on many occasions too, but in all the years I spent with her, nothing came close to the moment she unwrapped that Buddha. To say it meant the world to her would be an understatement of monumental proportions. From the day I brought it home to the day she passed away, that Buddha took top billing at her home. He now lives at *Juicy Oasis*, where my mum's magical energy lives on.

The point is that although this bit of magic making involved some money, it wasn't the *having* money that created this magical moment; it was, conversely, a *lack* of money. If I were a rich kid and had bought the Buddha, do you think for one second the same level of magic would have been created? Not in a million years. The reason this act of magic making created the deep level of magic it did was because my mum knew what it took for me to get it for her. And once again the reason for telling this story is, and no – I don't mind repeating it – you cannot create magic for others without creating it for yourself.

Not only did I get the magical moment of seeing my mum's face with rivers of happy tears pouring down it, but also if I ever did anything to make her proud of me, *I* immediately felt good. *The Joey Rule* is simply unavoidable when creating magic; there is always a benefit to you in some way, no matter how self*less* the magical act appears to be. The benefit might not always be glaringly obvious, but if you dig deep enough, you'll always find a secondary gain somewhere along the way. That secondary gain may simply be the avoidance of pain, but it's still a gain. There are some people who buy flowers for their partner, for example, not so much to create magic for them out of the blue, but sometimes to get themselves out of the doghouse!

CLICK TO BASKET

Again, this doesn't mean that money can't create huge amounts of magic, both for the individual and for others, because it clearly can, but sometimes simply 'clicking to basket' doesn't always cut the magic mustard. I can send my amazing nephew, Alfie, the latest Man United football kit by clicking to basket, or, I can try and make the effort to actually go and play football with him. Which do you think ultimately creates more magic? If I really can't go for whatever reason, then yes, clicking to basket will create *some* magic, but there are always ways to raise your magic game if you look for them. Take something as simple as a greeting card. Never underestimate the magic receiving a card through the post can create, especially when it's handwritten, genuine and thought has gone into what has been written. Those who know me know I am not a lover of e-cards, in fact I loathe them. I am also not a huge present-receiving person either, but I am a sucker for a genuinely thoughtful, handwritten card. Taking the time to buy and write a card is pretty much in everyone's grasp and it's possibly one of the easiest ways to create magic for people, especially when you send one for no other reason than to send love or just to say 'Hi!' In a world dominated by a screen of some kind, receiving a handwritten *real* card out of the blue, when it's not your birthday or Christmas, can turn a wintery day into a summer one in an instant and create more magic for someone than just clicking to basket.

FREE MAGIC

Then you have totally free magic. Some of the most magical moments I have ever experienced, either by myself or with others, have been free. Free magic is available to all of us and it's everywhere if you look for it. It's in a sunset, or a dip in the ocean, or a run in warm rain – it's different for all of us, but there's free magic all around us. We live in a time where we have access to millions of free books, films, galleries, museums, sunsets, clifftop views, star-filled skies, the list could go on and on. The point is, if your *money tree* is more of a shrub, don't use that as an excuse not to create magic. There's plenty of free magic out there and it's yours for the taking if you're willing to look for it. I cannot emphasise enough that the only thing really stopping you from creating magic is your imagination, not the size of your *money tree*.

THE MAGICAL POWERS OF THE MONEY TREE

Having said that, never underestimate the magical powers open to those who are either lucky enough, or have worked hard enough, to have a nice *money tree* in their garden. Not everyone with a decent *money tree* picks from it to create magic for others; some hang onto it for dear life. They think, wrongly, that if they let go of it, it will never return. The truth is money is like blood – it needs to flow to keep things alive. It needs to keep moving to create the magic it's capable of creating, not only for others, but also for you.

Some people with a big fat *money tree* understand this rule and, in many cases, the very reason they have money in the first place is *because* they've always understood this rule. If you interview virtually any self-made millionaire I guarantee they have always allowed money to flow, no matter how bare their *money tree* was to start with. I guarantee they were just as generous in using their money to create magic relative to what they had back then, as they are today. There are always exceptions to this rule and you will of course find people with big fat *money trees* who never pick from them to create magic, but they are without question much poorer for it. Richness isn't defined by money; it's a feeling. When you create magic, there's a richness in it that those who don't engage in magic making miss out on, no matter how much money they have. You show me a person who has a normal working wage but constantly looks for ways to create magic for others, and then show me a person with a forest of *money trees* but who hangs on to it for dear life, and I'll show you which one is ultimately richer. I think Charles Dickens' 1843 tale *A Christmas Carol* taught us all we need to know about the richness lost by hanging on to money. I don't think anyone would consider the main character, Scrooge, to have a rich life. He was financially rich but had no true richness in his world. We talk in this world of the 'haves' and 'have nots' mainly in reference to the size of people's money tree, but someone like Scrooge, despite his massive money tree, fell squarely into the 'have not' camp. The second he started using his wealth to create magic, he started to experience true richness in every area of his life.

Many multi-millionaires understand this principle and many use their vast wealth to create magic for people all the time, even if they're not singing it from the rooftops. Take the late and extremely talented George Michael for example. It wasn't until he passed away that stories of his incredible generosity came out. George was a magic maker, it was in his default and whenever he saw an opportunity to make magic, he took it. He gave millions to charities, but it was his random acts of magic that I love so much. He was once watching a game show called *Deal or No Deal*, where a contestant was hoping to win £15,000 to pay for IVF treatment. The top prize was £250,000, but she just needed £15,000 and set her sights on that. She didn't win and her dream of a child was shattered, until George stepped in of course. It's reported he called the show and gave her the money. I love this kind of magic making. It's spur of the moment and it's the kind of magic making that lifts your spirits. This is a perfect example of someone with a nice money tree picking from it often to create magic for someone he didn't even know and in doing so, because of *the Joey Rule*, created magic for himself.

What many people don't realise is that some of the wealthiest people on the planet are also some of the biggest magic makers in the world too. Bill Gates, Warren Buffet, Simon Cowell, Tony Robbins, Richard Branson and, at the time of writing this, the richest man in the world, Amazon founder Jeff Bezos announced a €2 billion fund to help homeless families and create pre-schools.

The One Day fund will support two charities, one for homeless families to provide shelter and hunger support and the other for creating high-quality, non-profit pre-schools in under-served communities. In part of a tweet he posted on the day of the announcement, Bezos said, 'Where's the good in the world and how can we spread it? Where are the opportunities to make things better? These are exciting questions.'

CLEVERNESS IS A GIFT, KINDNESS IS A CHOICE

When giving a talk at Princeton, Jeff told the grads, 'Cleverness is a gift, kindness is a choice', and I love that. Kindness is without question a choice we all have. Whether you have a big *money tree* or a tiny leafless shrub, we can all choose to be kind and create magic in order to help enrich the lives of others and ourselves. We might not all be able to set up a two-billion-dollar fund but we can all do *something*. We can all create magic in our own way with the time and resources *we* have at our own personal disposal. We all have the ability to tap into our imagination and explore different ways to create magic in every area of our lives.

There are way too many examples, to fit into this tiny book, of people with big *magic money trees* using them to create shed loads of magic for others. Whether it's Simon Cowell paying for a young girl's operation so she can walk again, Tony Robbins feeding millions of people a year or Richard Curtis doing more for children in Africa than most could possibly comprehend, the list of people with big *magic money trees* creating huge magic, mainly for strangers, is monumental. Most keep quiet about it, as George Michael did, choosing to simply get the magic of knowing they've helped someone. Others shout about it, not always to turn a halo on themselves, but often, to help create more magic for more people by bringing it into the public eye. One thing is clear though when it comes to the *magic money tree*, whether you have a small one or a forest full, we can all find ways to create magic in our own way. Never use lack of money as an excuse.

ANYONE CAN CREATE MAGIC!

There will of course be some people reading this who will no doubt go into the 'well it's easy for people with money to create magic' type of headspace, thinking, very wrongly, that you need money to create magic for others, or indeed for themselves. Make no mistake, money does give you more options to create magic, but sometimes all you need is....

TWENTY SECONDS OF COURAGE

5

One of my all-time favourite feel good movies is *We Bought A Zoo*. It's based on the true story of a man who lost his wife to cancer and the struggles he faced bringing up his son and daughter alone. As the title suggests, Benjamin Mee (the main character played by Matt Damon) ends up buying a zoo. You'll have to watch the movie to see how that came about and why it's such an uplifting feel-good movie, but the reason I mention the film here is because of one scene. In it, Benjamin is sitting on the floor talking to his son, having a heart-to-heart about a girl his son likes. The one nugget of advice he gives is this:

'You know sometimes, all you need is twenty seconds of insane courage. Literally, just twenty seconds of embarrassing bravery and I promise you, something great will come of it.'

'Twenty seconds of courage' is a wonderful concept to embrace in every area of life; this one concept alone can create more magic than you can comprehend. A personal example of this came one Thanksgiving evening on Santa Monica

beach in L.A. California. I was there for work but Thanksgiving was in the middle of it so I had a few days to myself. It was early morning and I was taking my daily long walk along the wonderful stretch of beach between the famous pier (which is also the end of Route 66) and Venice Beach. The weather was stunning, the sun was just rising and my feet were wet from the ocean. That in itself was a magical moment, but what happened next showed me you can create magic at the most unexpected times and places, providing you harness those *twenty seconds of courage*.

I noticed a woman, in her 50s or 60s, standing on the wet part of the sand staring out to sea. As I walked past her I sensed sadness and, as odd as this sounds, she looked like she needed a hug. She wasn't crying, but there was something that seemed to suggest a hug would do her the world of good. The problem is how on earth do you just go up to a stranger first thing in the morning on a beach when they are minding their own business and say 'You look like you need a hug.' So I walked past and continued my walk. When I turned around and headed back, I had to pass her again. She was still staring into the horizon with what seemed like true sadness in her gaze. I thought 'Come on Jason, just see if she's OK', but fear reared its head and I carried on walking. It's odd; put me on a stage to talk to 3,000 people and I have no nerves at all, but in this situation my heart was racing. I walked back again with the intention of asking her if she needed a hug, then as soon as I got near, I bottled it and carried on walking. I walked back and forth a few times before I realised I must have looked like a stalker! I then harnessed my *twenty seconds of courage* and thought, 'What's the worst that can happen?' If she doesn't need a hug and thinks I'm odd – no harm done and I'll be on my merry way; but if she does – it might make a huge difference to her day. I walked up to her and finally said, 'I'm really sorry to randomly come up to you and I know this seems really odd, but you look like you need a hug.' Within seconds she pulled me towards her and held me tighter than I have ever been held in my life. No words passed between us for several minutes, she just cried a lot. Eventually she managed to get some words out in-between the tears and said, 'My husband died six months ago and this is my first Thanksgiving without him.' At this point I also lost my crap and started crying with her. We held each other for a few more minutes while the tears flowed, and the embrace was still strong. She just kept saying, 'Thank you! Thank you! Thank you!' Eventually we unravelled from our embrace, stared at each other for a second, and I left.

To this day I have no idea who she is, where

she is, and in all likelihood, we'll never meet again. However, it was one of the most completely unplanned, wonderful '*create magic*' moments that I've ever experienced. I didn't ask myself that morning, 'How can I create magic for someone today?' I just saw her, felt her pain, used *twenty seconds of courage* to see if a hug would help and we both ended up experiencing a true moment of magic. It's actually hard to describe just how that moment felt, but there's an almost indescribable magic in it, a magic that simply buying somebody something could rarely, if ever, match.

Twenty seconds of courage is a magnificent tool, which can create more magic in every single area of your life. Chances come and go and even just harnessing twenty seconds of this most precious commodity can be the difference between taking those chances and letting them simply slip away. *Twenty seconds of courage* can get you the relationship, which may otherwise have passed you by. *Twenty seconds of courage* can get you the career or business of your dreams.*Twenty seconds of courage* can get you to travel the world, to be adventurous, to try things you never have. *Twenty seconds of courage* can get you to open up, to tell people you love them, to connect in ways that may have previously never happened. Tapping into *twenty seconds of insane courage* can be the difference between creating immeasurable amounts of magic for you, and possibly others, or none at all. But I feel the real beauty of *twenty seconds of courage* is that it can create even unexpected and monumental magic even in something as small as a hug on a beach with a stranger.

Now, you've seen how tapping into your *twenty seconds of courage* can create unexpected magical connections wherever you go, there is a type of magic that has the power to bring even more magic to your world. It's what I describe as...

A *STRANGER* KIND OF MAGIC

6

As illustrated by hugging a complete stranger, creating magic for someone you don't know has the power to enrich your world more than you can possibly imagine. It lifts the spirits in such a beautiful way and makes an immediate positive impact on someone else's world. It has the ability to restore a person's faith in humanity and can cause a magical ripple effect that will be felt for years to come. There's a truly special kind of magic when you create magic for a stranger and there are hundreds of opportunities to indulge in this wonderful practice almost daily. It could be something as small as giving up your seat on a bus or buying a coffee for someone living on the street, all the way to buying a stranger a car. Creating magic for strangers is open to everyone.

We now live in a time where even if you don't personally have access to a large *magic money tree*, you have immediate access to a world of good people who do. People who, when reached out to in the right way and with the right story, want nothing more than to help create magic for people less fortunate. As I have said throughout the book, and will no doubt be repeating again, it's not a lack of money that prevents most people from creating magic, it's a lack of imagination. It's also a lack of a strong enough reason to create magic. You'll be amazed at how incredibly resourceful most people are if they have a strong, compelling reason behind their magic making.

Take Sean and Darilyn Merrill who created magic for a stranger using the power of their imagination, not their money. The Merrills stopped at a red light and saw a middle-aged man, Robert Ford, walking across the road directly in front of their car. It was 9.45pm and the man seemed tired and was walking with a lunch box in his hand and his head was down. Sean said, 'I felt a strong urge to stop and ask him if he needed a ride. My wife agreed so I pulled over.' Robert explained to the couple that he'd missed the bus that day, and that it usually took him two and a half hours on public transport to get to work. After dropping off the stranger, they came up with a plan, and set up a GoFundMe account in a bid to raise enough money to buy Robert a car. To cut a long story short, this amazing couple managed to not only raise enough to buy this stranger a car, but also enough to pay for the insurance. Sean said:

> *'I think it's important to take a step back and think about others and think about the fact they*

are a person just like you. They go through the same struggles, maybe different experiences, but everyone needs help now and again.'

By help he clearly means magic. Everyone needs a little magic now and then and when that magic comes from total strangers, it somehow makes it even more special. The real beauty though, because of the philosophy of magic making, is that it won't stop there. Magic *creates* magic and the *ripple of magic* from this event will be felt for a long time to come. The stranger, Robert, summed this up when he said:

'I owe them a lot, and I'm going to do my best to help somebody else.'

This story made the news late in 2015, and there's no question its magical ripples are being felt to this day. There have since been quite a few examples of similar magic being created for strangers and I'm sure one of the reasons it's happening is down to these incredible stories. One of the most powerful I've read has to be that of Andy Mitchell and the fast-food worker.

Andy spotted a young man in a fast food uniform walking along the side of a road on a 95-degree summer's day in Rockwell, Texas. He noticed the guy was melting in the heat so he pulled over and offered 20-year-old Justin Korva a lift. He discovered that Justin walked three miles to work and three miles home every day. Justin said he was determined to save up enough money one day to buy himself a car. After dropping him at work, Andy posted all about Justin's determination on Facebook:

> *'To all the people that say they want to work but can't find a job or don't have a vehicle, all I can say is you don't want it bad enough.'*

Hundreds saw the post and in less than 48 hours, with a nice donation from Andy himself, $5,500 was raised. A general sales manager at the local Toyota garage also saw the post and told his boss, who hugely reduced the price on a Toyota Camry. Not only was there enough money to buy the car, but there was enough left over for two years' worth of oil changes and a $500 petrol card. The guys from the garage and Andy Mitchell drove the car to Taco Casa, where Justin worked, and presented him with it. 'Justin, you can't imagine all the people who wanted to help you', explained Andy, 'So instead of walking to work, buddy, you're driving this car from now on.' Justin looked at Mitchell in disbelief and said, 'Are you serious?' To which Andy kept having to repeat, 'It's your car! This is *your* car!'

Take the story of the students who raised enough money to send one of their university cleaners on holiday to Jamaica. This proves again that money really is no object when it comes to creating magic. Herman Gordon, a 65-year-old cleaner had worked at Bristol University for 12 years. He was moved to tears when the students there raised £1500 for his trip. The money meant Herman, who was part of the Windrush generation, was able to return to his hometown for the first time in years.

The students who gave him the money said:

> *'All year round, this man works hours on end to provide us with a clean working space in which to study. But most importantly, his undying positive energy and chit-chat has managed to turn many students' dark days into positive ones filled with joy. Whether you're just feeling generally down and out or stressed out due to exams, Herman is always there to speak to you.'*

These students, along with people like Andy Mitchell and Sean and Darilyn Merrill, may not have had their own huge *magic money tree* to pick from to create instant magic, but they did have the two most important commodities required for genuine magic making – imagination and a *genuine* desire to want to make a difference. The truth is, if you really want to create magic for a stranger, even if it seems too big in the moment

– like buying them a car – there is always a way if you're committed. What I also love about both of these stories is that the people who received the magic weren't just sitting at home watching junk TV and bitching about why the Universe was not providing for them. They were out there doing what *they* could so that the Universe could meet them half-way!

UNPLANNED MAGIC

When it comes to creating magic for strangers, clearly you don't have to buy someone a car. It's often the tiniest acts that have the most impact. When you create any kind of magic for a total stranger, it blindsides them, which is one of the beauties of it. The general rule of magic making is the more it blindsides someone, the greater the intensity of magic that is created. This is why, even what looks on the surface to be a small insignificant gesture, can often have a very large impact on someone. The vast majority of the magic you'll create for strangers will be unplanned. It will be in the moment, when you're out and about or you see a post online and have this immediate driving desire to create a little magic for someone. It's like when I was in Santa Monica, I didn't plan on hugging a random stranger that day; it was in the moment, totally unplanned, and it just felt like the right thing to do. As it turned out it created more magic for all concerned than I ever imagined possible and to this day, it will remain one of the most memorable experiences of my life. Whether it's helping to pay for someone's shopping when you see they've not got enough money at the checkout, or helping someone to cross the road, or just nipping into a florist, buying a bunch of flowers and randomly giving them to a stranger to lift their day, wanting to create magic for a stranger often just washes over you in the moment and I encourage you to seize those moods and moments wherever possible.

Take the story of George Michael I told earlier, the one where he created magic for a woman who didn't win enough money on the gameshow for her IVF treatment. He didn't *plan* to create magic for anyone that day, he was simply chilling at home watching a bit of *Deal Or No Deal*, saw this woman's plight and called in and gave her the money.

It was this story that influenced my decision to do something similar last year. I was watching *This Morning* and there was a man who called into their daily phone in who had lost his job. It was just before Christmas and he didn't want to tell his wife because he was worried about letting her and his young son down. He was extremely upset and you could hear his voice shaking as he spoke. It's hard to convey just how moving the phone call was, but in the style of George Michael I got in touch with the programme and gave him some money to help him over the Christmas hump. I wasn't doing a completely selfless good deed; remember truly selfless good deeds don't exist. I did it because I knew it would create a bit of Christmas magic all round, *including* for myself. This was the first email I received from him:

> *'Good evening Jason. I really, really cannot believe this is happening, I really can't. From the bottom of my heart I mean it thank you. I can really have a good Christmas with my family and most of all my son, I really can't describe what this means to me.'*

He has written to me a few times since, including a truly lovely message on Christmas Day itself, which was just magical. He and his family not only had a great Christmas but he managed to get back to work in the New Year. The point is creating magic for this total stranger made *me* feel stupidly good and if anyone should take the credit for this bit of magic making it should be George Michael. I would never have thought about contacting a TV show to help someone who called in if I hadn't heard the story about George Michael doing it. This is why the golden rule of creating magic is solid and why once you start a magic snowball, it's almost impossible to stop it.

You also have no idea what your kind gesture of magic will eventually turn into.

A BASKET FULL OF MAGIC

Take perhaps the biggest magic snowball ever created by a random stranger. It all started with a knock on the door at the home of Tony Robbins one Thanksgiving. Tony was only a young boy at the time and on this day of feasting, his mum and dad were wondering how they would even scrape together a basic meal. His parents were extremely proud people, and although they could have contacted a local charity that would have supplied a turkey and all the trimmings, his parents would rather make do with what they had than accept charity. Tensions ran high on the day and harsh words were exchanged as the stress of not being able to have a normal Thanksgiving took its toll. Tony said he felt devastated and helpless as he watched the people he loved most become more and more angry and depressed. However, everything was about to change with a loud and unexpected knock on the door. Tony opened the door and was greeted by a tall man carrying a huge basket brimming with every conceivable Thanksgiving indulgence: a turkey, stuffing, pies, sweet potatoes, canned goods and more. The man at the door said, 'This is from someone who knows you're in need and wants you to know that you're loved and cared for.' Tony's proud father didn't want to take the basket, but the man said, 'Look, I'm just a delivery person.' With a big smile on his face, he set the basket in the boy's arms, turned to leave, then called over his shoulder, 'Have a great Thanksgiving!'

It was a moment that would ultimately change the lives of millions of people all over the world. It was a moment that started a magical snowball. Tony was so moved by this act of kindness from a total stranger, and swore to himself that someday he'd do well enough to give something back to others in a similar situation.

By the time he was eighteen, he had already started to fulfil that promise. With his small earnings, he went and bought some groceries, not for himself, but for two families he'd heard were in dire need of some food. Dressed in an old pair of jeans and a T-shirt to give the impression he was just the delivery boy, he knocked on the first house. A Latina woman who had six children greeted him with suspicion. Tony said, 'I have a delivery for you ma'am.' He then went to his car and started to carry in boxes full of food: a turkey, stuffing, pies, sweet potatoes, canned goods and more. The same wonderful basket full of goodies a random stranger had delivered to him and his family on Thanksgiving only a few years earlier. The woman's jaw dropped and the children, when they saw what was happening, let out shrieks of delight. The woman only spoke in broken English but kissed Tony all over his face and said 'You're a gift from God', to which Tony simply replied 'No, no! I'm just the delivery boy. This is a gift from a friend.' Tony then handed her a note that said:

> *'This is a note from a friend. Please have a wonderful Thanksgiving – you and your family deserve it. Know that you are loved. And someday, if you have the chance, please do well enough to do this for someone else and pass on the gift.'*

You never know where your kind gestures will ultimately lead. You never know the size of magic snowball you may have started. The stranger who created magic for Tony and his family couldn't possibly have ever imagined it would lead to millions of people getting fed, not only on Thanksgiving, but now throughout the whole year. The stranger knocked on the door of a young Tony Robbins, a boy who would grow up and go on to become the world's leading self-development coach and magic maker extraordinaire. Tony kicked things off with The Basket Brigade, where people from all over the world replicate the Thanksgiving magic that the stranger created for him and his family. The Basket Brigade is now a global feeding movement that provides help for families all year around. Tony has now helped to feed a billion people in need, that's *one billion people*! That's magic making on such an epic scale that it's hard to get your head around. A copy of Tony's magic-making book, *Notes From A Friend* is often provided too. The book encourages people to do the same for someone else, just like the note Tony received on that life-changing Thanksgiving Day encouraged him to. Taking that element into account, one can only imagine the true number of people this original basket of magic has gone on to help. Tony goes one stage further by providing them with key, simple psychological tools in his book – tools that will give them a better fighting chance of doing well enough in life to be able to do the same for someone else. Tony doesn't simply want to give some food, he wants to educate and inspire so people can lift themselves out of their current position and make their life more magical. His drive comes from a genuine desire to want to make a massive difference and create obscene amounts of magic. From what I see, Tony is not in the self-development business, but is in the pure magic-making business.

THE ART OF LIVING IS GIVING

One of Tony's teachings is *The Art Of Living Is Giving* and he walks his talk on a massive scale. Most of his magic making, like that of many in the public eye who have generated large *magic money trees*, is off radar. However, he practices the art of giving daily and the ripples are felt all over the world.

TAKING MAGIC MAKING TO ANOTHER LEVEL

When it comes to creating magic for strangers, there's a level of magic making that goes way beyond anything money can ever buy. To give your money is one thing but to give something of yourself, *literally*, is a whole different magical ball game. Every day, there are people giving blood to help save the lives of strangers all over the world, a magical act that is within the reach of most of us. The human body is pure magic in itself and the blood you give will soon regenerate and ultimately, you'll lose nothing but your time. However, there are other acts of magic making where people give something of themselves, again literally, but never get it back. I'm talking specifically here about organ donation. A kind of magic that transforms and saves lives each and every day. When it comes to organ donation, it's one thing to agree to donate your organs once you've died, but to agree to give an organ to a stranger while you're still alive is magic making on a level most of us can't comprehend.

Geoff Kennedy, from Nova Scotia, gave one of his kidneys to a total stranger after seeing his plea on social media. Rob Edwards, a 38-year-old married father of two young boys had been waiting for a kidney for four years to replace the one a genetic disease was destroying. Geoff, whose own father was given a second chance at life with a double lung transplant, saw the post, got tested, found he was a match and donated his kidney. After the operation he said the huge outpouring of support touched him. His act seemed to have restored a lot of people's faith in humanity. When asked if he was worried about the risks he simply said, 'It was the right thing to do.' Since then he has heard from friends who have signed up to donate blood for the first time and from one friend who reached out to give their own kidney to someone who needed it. This is the beauty of the *ripple of magic* effect. In this case Geoff Kennedy has caused a life-saving *ripple of magic*. Giving blood may have seemed like a big deal before, but after Geoff's friends saw he gave a kidney, giving blood all of a sudden didn't seem like such a big deal. His unbelievable act of magic making for a total stranger will go on to save way more lives than just the man he gave his kidney to. Geoff of course isn't alone, there are many stories of people giving organs to random strangers and saving their lives. Once again though, and this will be harder to get your head around than in other examples in this book, these are still not totally selfless good deeds. They are monumentally good deeds, but not totally selfless. Once again it makes the person giving the organ feel good. In Geoff's case, I'm imagining it made him feel amazing! Not only was his own father's life saved by a donor, so it was a way of repaying the favour to some extent, but also saving a total stranger's life must have brought a personal type of magic most of us will never experience.

ALL MAGIC IS MAGICAL

Whether it's giving a stranger a basket of food, a hug or even something as monumental as a kidney, *all* magic making for strangers has the power to truly enrich your life on so many levels. It restores people's faith in humanity and, as you've seen, has the ability to create a magical snowball that's often unstoppable.

THE BIG THREE!

When it comes to magic making, there are three fundamental areas where, if you practice the art of it, you will enrich your life beyond measure. This is why I have dedicated a mini chapter to each one. First up is perhaps arguably the most important of all...

YOUR *RELATIONSHIP* WITH MAGIC

7

If you are in a relationship and you don't regularly ask the question, 'How can I create magic for my partner?' don't be surprised if you experience the biggest relationship magic trick of them all – the one where your relationship totally disappears! If you're not in a relationship, but really want to be, and you don't ask yourself, 'How can I create magic for my date?' every time you go on one, don't be surprised if your dates don't come back for seconds!

Now before I continue on this mini relationship chapter, you need to know I am not putting myself up there as a relationship expert. Personally, I don't think anyone can claim to be an expert in this field; there are simply far too many variables and relationships can often be complicated. However, one thing is for sure, if you want to prevent your partner vanishing before your very eyes, you must find ways to create magic, *consistently*. This doesn't mean every five minutes or even daily – I explain why you shouldn't do this fully in the *Don't Dilute The Magic* chapter as that can also backfire and kill the magic. However, throughout your relationship you need to regularly find ways to add a little magic to proceedings. I say you cannot stop creating magic because I bet my bottom dollar that if you go back to the start of any relationship, magic would have been flying about all over the place.

People have no problem thinking of ways to create magic at the *start* of a relationship, mainly because they're essentially auditioning for the part of becoming someone's partner and getting the full-time role. Flowers are bought, restaurants are booked, presents are given, cute cards are written, homemade candlelit dinners are the norm and stories are told *and* listened to. Sensual massages are given, sexy underwear is worn, log fires are lit, weekends away are booked, films are watched while you are tucked up under the same blanket, new clothes are bought, grooming is done, there's genuine magic in the air and all is good in the relationship world. Where it goes wrong is when creating magic stops. When the cute handwritten cards become history, the cheeky messages on the whiteboard are replaced with to-do lists, the naughty weekends are suddenly second fiddle to weekends away with friends, candlelit dinners are substituted for microwave meals in front of the TV, sexy underwear is a distant memory, and stories are told but no longer listened to. The very magic that made the relationship so exciting, attractive, amazing and electric slowly dwindles and you're both left in a largely magic-free relationship wondering what the hell happened.

Nine times out of ten, only one thing happened: either you, them, or both of you, stopped finding ways to create magic for each other. Clearly, there are times when a relationship will end no matter how much magic someone throws at it: it may have run its course, or you may have gone in completely different directions, but the chances of staying in a fulfilling, loving, exciting relationship for longer goes up a thousand-fold if you find ways to *consistently* create magic. Obviously, it must be a two-way street. If you constantly create magic for your partner and no magic of any kind ever comes back from them to you, then they shouldn't be surprised if you do a vanishing act.

DOUBLE THE MAGIC

When it comes to creating magic for your partner, experiencing a double dose of magic for yourself is almost inevitable. You not only get the magic of knowing you've done something lovely for someone you love (no such thing as a selfless good deed and all that) but when it comes to creating magic for your partner, you often get to experience the same magic too and thus get double the dose. You book a cheeky weekend away, you get to go too. You cook a nice dinner with some fine wine – you get to enjoy it too. You give your partner a massage – you get to caress their beautiful naked body. You get tickets to a West End show – you get to go too. That's the added bonus of creating magic in a relationship, you often get to experience the very same magic you've created for your partner.

THE MAGIC OF UNCONDITIONAL LOVE

Magic making in *all* your relationships is important if you want them to be long lasting, fulfilling and rich in nature, but when it comes to your most intimate one it's often essential for its very survival. Relationships with your family usually come with the luxury of unconditional love, not in every case, but in most. This is a special kind of love which means exactly that, *unconditional*. Even if there's no magic making going on, you all still love each other. You may not *like* each other at times, but the unconditional love is blood-rich and as solid as oak. This doesn't mean that some family relationships don't break down completely, because boy, they do, but when a family relationship hits the rocks, it usually isn't caused by a lack of creating *magic*, but rather it will be a case of someone in the family creating *tragic*.

Genuine unconditional love is the type of love usually only found in family relationships. It's the kind of love rarely, if ever, found in intimate relationships; which is why, if you want your relationship to last, it's imperative you think about creating magic on a regular basis. You may feel that's not the case, that most relationships have unconditional love, but the truth is there are always conditions when it comes to an intimate relationship. The 'I will love you no matter what' mantra is a lovely sentiment, but it doesn't hold a great deal of sway in loving relationship land. The 'I will love you...*no matter what*' is really more a case of 'I will love you... *providing you do this and don't do that.*' Monogamy, for example, for the vast majority of intimate relationships is a very, *very* clear condition. The 'I love you no matter what' soon goes out the window if you're found sleeping with their best friend!

The hard truth is that pure *unconditional* love is not something usually found in intimate relationships, there are always some conditions. Those conditions will be different for everyone but show me any intimate relationship and I guarantee there will be conditions attached. This is not a bad thing – it keeps us on our relationship toes – but without question, whether we are conscious of it or not, creating magic for each other on a regular basis is one of those main conditions.

KEEPING THE MAGIC FIRE BURNING

Magic is kindling to a relationship, it's the very thing that ignites the spark and helps to keep the relationship fire burning bright. When you hear people saying their relationship has lost its spark, what they really mean is the relationship has lost its magic. To be more precise, what they really mean is either they, their partner or both of them have stopped creating magic. You cannot expect your relationship to maintain the magic if *you're* not doing anything to create it. In the words of JFK:

'Ask not what your relationship can do for you; but what you can do for your relationship.'

And what you can do above everything else to keep it fresh, fun, loving, exciting and alive is to keep the magic flag flying by creating magic wherever and whenever you can.

As I write this book, I have been in a relationship with my Katie for almost fourteen years. Katie is one of life's natural born magic makers. Creating magic isn't something she has to work hard to perfect, because it's her default. It's who she is, it's what she does and it's in her DNA. It's something she has consistently done throughout our entire relationship, not just something she did in the first few months. It's not a one-way '*create magic*' relationship either – if it were I'd have been out on my ear a long time ago. Creating magic in a relationship has to be a two-way street. Like Katie, I also have '*create magic*' DNA (which I think I inherited from my magic-making mum) and do what I can to consistently create magic throughout our relationship. We do this not because we *have* to, but because we *want* to. Magic breeds magic and it feels good to create and receive magic – especially when it involves someone you love. If your partner creates some cool magic for you, it makes you want to create even more magic for them. As I have said, if you look for ways to create magic in your intimate relationship the chances of having a more fulfilling, adventurous, loving and lasting one goes up quite a few notches. I don't know if Katie and I will be together forever; I'd like to believe so as I feel my world would crumble without this amazing woman, but no one has a crystal ball. What I do know is the chance of happily ever after with Katie goes up *considerably* if neither of us drops the magic-making ball – complacency in a relationship is the biggest killer.

When it comes to creating magic in an intimate relationship, there are a billion different ways to do it. As with all magic making, no matter which part of your life you're looking at, you're limited not so much by the size of your *magic money tree*, but rather the size of your imagination. In a relationship, it can often be the smallest gestures that create the most magic. It can come in the form of a hug or a kiss delivered at just the right time, or in a simple handwritten card left under the pillow before you head to work. It can come in the form of a cheeky message on the whiteboard on the fridge, or breakfast in bed. Only *you* will know what can create magic for your partner. It's about listening to them, knowing what makes *them* tick, and understanding what would be magical for *them*.

Creating magic within a relationship needs a balance of little sprinkles of magic – like a surprise candlelit bubble bath with a cheeky glass of fizz – to big moments of magic that take their breath away, move someone emotionally and sweep them off their feet. The little sprinkles of magic should be spread evenly on a fairly regular basis, whereas the big magic should be reserved for now and then. The big magic only happens when something is unexpected, takes them by surprise and moves them emotionally. Big magic is the kind of magic that takes the breath away. What's important to know is you cannot and should not try to create big magic all the time. All that happens, if you attempt to do this, is that you'll dilute the magic and whatever you're doing will stop being magical. You need to use your powers wisely in order for them to retain the magic-making impact you're looking for.

MAGIC AT 35,000FT

Talking of big magic, a few years ago I took my Katie on holiday to Mexico for Valentine's Day. We were extremely lucky to have shed loads of air miles with Virgin and so had the luxury of travelling in Upper Class. Valentine's fell on the day we were flying back, and we were on the redeye. Before we even left the UK, I asked myself, 'How can I create some big magic on Valentine's Day?' As we'd be travelling that day, I couldn't arrange a candlelit dinner — or could I? It dawned on me that I could create magic at 35,000ft and have a Valentine's meal to remember. I bought some electric candles, wrote a card and hid them away in my hand luggage. As we boarded the plane, I took one of the cabin crew to one side and told them what I had planned. As Virgin is naturally in the magic-making business, they were fully on board and happy to help in any way they could. Just to paint the picture, on Virgin Upper you can effectively sit opposite each other for dinner, if you choose. So I asked them to set the table for two, turn on the candles, pour the champagne, and rest the card next to Katie's glass. I then leaned over to Katie's seat and asked if she'd like to join me for a candlelit Valentine's meal for two at 35,000ft. The Virgin crew added a few little magic bits themselves, which all helped to make it pretty special. The entire trip was already firmly in the big-magic territory, but there are always ways to raise the game even further if you search for them. This isn't me being the big 'I am' because it wasn't a completely selfless good deed, it never is. In this case, I got double the magic, which I have said often happens when it comes to creating magic in your relationship. I got the magic of feeling good knowing I'd done something special for the person I love, but I also got the magic of having a Valentine's 'candlelit' dinner in the sky – something that will probably never happen again in my life.

Clearly, you don't need Virgin Upper – or anything of that magnitude – to create big magic. My Katie proved this early on in our relationship when she surprised me with tickets to a play at the Minack Theatre in Cornwall. To this day it's one of the most magical dates I've ever been on and, for me, it completely dwarfs my 'candlelit' dinner six miles up! The Minack Theatre is one of the most unique theatres in the world and is magical in its own right. It's an open-air theatre, and the seats are all carved into the rock face with the sea is just behind where the action takes place. Katie had brought a blanket, a small bottle of bubbly, some champagne flutes and a couple of Cornish pasties. In an unplanned piece of added magic, the moon rose from the ocean and lit up the sea like a Christmas tree. It was the kind of night that took your breath away and was pure, for want of a better word, magic. The Minack Theatre isn't expensive and Cornish pasties hardly break the bank, but the magic created was huge. For me, it was *far* bigger than the seemingly more expensive Virgin dinner. This is why, as I keep repeating, your ability to create big magic is not reliant on the size of your *magic money tree* but more on your imagination. That's not to say that having the benefit of a fruitful *magic money tree* growing in your back-yard doesn't give you more options and ways to expand your magic-making imagination, but you don't *need* one.

CRAZY - SEXY - MAGIC

I feel we can't talk about creating magic in relationships without bringing sex into the mix. For some sex is more important than for others, but I think it's safe to say for the majority of people, sex plays a major role in relationships. I also think it's fair to say if you lose the magic in the bedroom, you've lost a huge part of the magic in the whole relationship.

Everyone's sex drive, desires, and fantasies are different and what may be magical for you in-between the sheets may not be your partner's cup of tea (different strokes for different folks, and all that!) So, when it comes to sex, the chances of you having *exactly* the same sex drive, desires and fantasies as your partner is quite rare. This doesn't mean you can't have a cracking sex life or an extremely compatible sex life, but it does mean there may be some differences in sexual exploration opinions. This is why – when thinking of ways to create magic for your partner on the sex front – it may not always involve the same level of sexual magic for you, or any at all, for that matter.

TAKING ME UP THE SHARD!

A perfect example of this was when my Katie 'took me up The Shard' (no this is not a euphemism, I mean The Shard in London – but I like saying Katie took me up the Shard so thought I'd include it here because I've never really grown up! ☺) The extremely unique piece of sexual magic making I am about to share happened in-between one Christmas and New Year. I opened a Christmas card on the big day and the gift of an overnight stay at the Shangri-La; a meal at the breathtaking restaurant at the top of the Shard itself; and a Christmas show at the Old Vic Theatre popped out along with a beautiful message. Now, all of this magic has the beauty of the double-magic rule, which often happens when creating magic in a relationship. Katie not only gets to experience the instant magic by knowing she's completely blown me away with an incredible gift, but she also got to stay at the stunning hotel, eat at the amazing top floor restaurant with its breathtaking views across London, and of course, she got to enjoy the show too. However, the added piece of magic that was also written in the card was, without question, *purely* for me. It is not the kind of magic most people would create for their partners, but then Katie isn't most people. Admittedly I had to re-read it a few times and ask many times, 'Are you f—king kidding me?' (in a very good way may I add) to make sure it wasn't a joke.

Now, before I let you into this very private piece of sexual magic that Katie created for me, let me tell you the circumstances that led to it. After several rounds of IVF, Katie was lucky enough to fall pregnant. Because it was an IVF baby, the clinic had told her she shouldn't fly or have sex for the first three months. Katie had wanted a child more than anything else in the world and, given how hard it was to get pregnant and given she had already experienced a miscarriage the year before, she was understandably extremely fearful of anything going wrong. She was of the mindset (and who can blame her) that if it was potentially harmful to fly in the first three months, flying might pose a risk at any time during the pregnancy. So, she made the decision not to fly while pregnant. Unfortunately for me, she also applied the same rule to sex, which was well and truly off the table for the whole pregnancy! However, Katie being the magic-making human she is, didn't see why her going off sex should mean no sexual experience of any kind for me too. So, as well as the meal, the play and the stay at the stunning hotel for Christmas, she also thought she'd create some sexual magic by getting me a Tantric massage in the hotel room. When the masseuse arrived, Katie picked up her book and said, 'I'll be upstairs reading, having a nice cup of tea and looking at London by night – enjoy!' Now that is magic making on another level.

There may well, of course, be some reading this who might jump into judgmental mode, but as Madonna famously said:

'Poor is the person whose pleasures depend on the permission of another.'

I appreciate it takes a certain kind of person to create that kind of sexual magic for their partner, but one of the reasons I believe our relationship has lasted so long is because we don't get caught up with the often crippling jealousy that plagues so many relationships. I have surprised Katie in very similar ways over the years and we love to create sexual magic for each other, in whatever way, shape or form that may come in.

We are living in the freest, most exciting and non-judgmental era of sexual liberation in history, so creating sexual magic within a relationship is only limited by your imagination. Like any area of life, there needs to be adventure and exploration to keep it alive, exciting and fresh. The problem is very few people have honest and open dialogue when it comes to sex in a relationship and very few constantly look for ways to create magic in this area, especially the longer the relationship goes on. Given how important sex is to the majority of intimate relationships, it's not an area you want to skimp and scrape on when it comes to magic making. The reality is, the *longer* a relationship goes on the *more* important it is to be open to creating new kinds of sexual magic for each other.

We also need to understand that sexual magic is different for everyone, but if you want your relationship to remain alive in the bedroom department, it's important to be honest about what floats *your* individual sexual boats. You may think you already know what your partner wants, but that might be based on where you guys were when you first met. Things change, desires change, fantasies change and what made you or your partner wild with excitement a few years ago may well not do the same thing now. It's important to move with personal sexual times and communicate what you'd love to experience. It's vital for the health and longevity of a relationship to keep sexual adventures alive.

THE MAGIC OF SEXUAL OPENNESS

As I said, the new sexual exploration desires your partner has may not always be fully in line with yours, just as *your* new sexual desires may not be in line with *theirs*, but so what? This shouldn't mean you both can't be free to explore them. Throughout a long-term relationship it's unlikely you'll always want to eat the same dinner or watch the same film, but then again so what? Sometimes we'll compromise and watch a film that wouldn't have been either of our first choices, but we still enjoy it; or we'll share a meal that wasn't top of the menu, but again, we still enjoy it. The point is it's not unusual for our sexual desires to not always align one hundred per cent, but by knowing what floats your partner's boat you have a much better chance of blowing their mind by creating some amazing sexual magic. This doesn't mean compromising your own personal sexual integrity; obviously don't just blindly create their sexual magic if it's something you genuinely hate or resent. What I'm talking about is letting go of judgement and jealousy where possible in order to create some seriously magical sexual adventure!

THE MAGICAL DATING GAME

Of course, before you even think about creating magic in a relationship, you have to be in one. I realise that being in a committed relationship isn't everyone's idea of magic, but for the majority of people not in one, most would at least like to try some committed, intimate magic on for size. And when it comes to attracting that special person there have never been more ways of finding 'the one'. However, there has also never been as much competition either, so if you want to stand out from the crowd, a little dating magic can often make all the difference. If you're really committed to finding a long-term love and connection, you need to be on your magic A game every time you go on a date. You need to think differently, set yourself apart from the rest and shake things up. Again, this is only limited by your imagination, and it doesn't take much to add some magic to dating proceedings.

Take something as simple as meeting someone for a drink in a pub. Most people simply turn up, looking their best, sit down and chew the dating fat over a drink. Nothing wrong with this at all, but it's not different; it doesn't do anything to mix up the dating game and make you stand out. How beautifully different would it be if, instead of staying in the pub, you had a cool bag with a nice bottle of champagne, a couple of champagne flutes, some lovely snacks, a huge rug, and took them over to the park instead? There are so many wonderful places, with amazing views that don't cost a penny; all it takes is a little imagination. I used a park as an example because many years ago I once organised sushi to be delivered to the middle of St James's Park in London for a date. It was a beautiful, sunny evening and what better place to eat dinner than in my favourite park in the world, just a stone's throw from Buckingham Palace. Just so you know, back then creating this kind of magic wasn't easy. Smartphones, social media and things like Uber Eats just didn't exist. I called Yo Sushi from my massive mobile phone that resembled a brick and asked if they'd deliver...to the middle of the park! This was a very unusual request but I told them roughly where I'd be, gave my number and told them a time to deliver. I went for a walk with my date in the park and asked if she wanted to go to dinner. I found a spot in the middle of the park, with a beautiful view of the pond and laid out a large blanket. I cracked open a bottle of bubbles and she said, 'I thought we were going for some sushi?', to which I replied, 'No, the sushi is coming to us!' At which point I saw the little Yo Sushi bike on the road in the distance and ran over to get the order. It was one of the best dates and what's great was creating a little more magic than simply going to a crowded, noisy sushi bar with no view.

And that's the beauty of asking yourself 'How can I create magic?' before going on a date, as it opens up so many different possibilities. If you live in a major city like London, Paris or New York, there are thousands of places at your disposal to help you raise your dating game, and they're free! Actually, no matter where you are, there are usually many wonderful spaces you can use. I'd go as far as to say some of the most magical places to share a bite to eat and a cheeky glass of bubbles are places you don't need to book a table at. Parks, beaches, clifftops, rooftop restaurants, iconic monuments, the list is endless.

AT THE STRIKE OF MAGIC

I remember for one of my first dates with my Katie, I used London's most iconic bell to create some magic. The night of our date fell on the eve of her birthday. I didn't really know her that well, and we weren't in a relationship of any kind at this point, but I knew the stroke of midnight would officially be the start of her birthday and so I wanted to create some special magic. I tried to time it so we'd leave the restaurant, walk along London's South Bank and hit the pedestrian bridge to the right of Westminster Bridge just in time for Big Ben to chime at midnight. I couldn't have timed it better! Just as we got halfway across the bridge, I stopped, waited for the chimes, kissed her and wished her a happy birthday. That was our first kiss and a truly special moment. One thing is for sure, create some added magic on a date and your chances of making a better connection go up considerably. The night was crisp and clear, the London Eye was beautifully lit to our left, Big Ben and the Houses of Parliament were to our right as we looked out across the Thames, the moon lit up the river and all combined to create a very magical moment. The point is, I didn't build the London Eye, or Big Ben, nor did I have anything to do with the moon or the Thames, but they all came into play to create some magic. The cost of this particular magical moment – zero! You can take someone to the most pretentious restaurant you've had to book months in advance and not create anywhere near as much magic. Use what's around you, think differently and stand out from the crowd by creating some magic on every date you go on.

As I have said, most people *start* their relationships creating magic all over the place, but before you know it complacency sets in and the magic vanishes. If you want a relationship full of magic all you have to do is keep finding ways to create it.

I mentioned there are three main areas in life where a '*create magic*' mindset is vital if you want to be successful. We've just explored the first one, *Your Relationship With Magic*, now on to the second one that has the power to bring even more magic into your world. It's what I describe as...

THE *BUSINESS* OF CREATING MAGIC

8

If you're in any kind of business, or you work for a business, to be truly successful you need to be in the business of creating magic. You need to be thinking about ways to create magic for your customers, your team, the business itself and for you personally.

YOU DON'T WORK FOR YOUR BOSS, YOU WORK FOR YOU AND THE PEOPLE YOU SERVE

One thing I realised early on in my working life was that ultimately, I didn't work for whoever owned the company. I worked for me. I worked for my family and I worked for the people I was ultimately serving. That doesn't mean I didn't want to impress my boss, or get recognition for what I did, but those things took second fiddle to *wanting* to do a good job for *me*. I took pride in whatever I did, no matter what I did. I wanted work to be as productive, rewarding and as fun as possible, and I also wanted to bring a little magic into the workplace wherever I could. I was always extremely grateful for the opportunity to do whatever job I was doing, which I believe is the single most important aspect of making your working world more magical. I was always grateful to whoever employed me and for the purpose it gave me.

When it comes to work, boy, have I done my fair share of diverse jobs over the years. I have worked on markets, as a tyre fitter, a butcher, a roofer, a labourer, in a video rental store, in a factory, as a delivery driver, a caterer (I use that term very loosely!), I've bought and sold cars, I've bought and sold furniture; you name it, I may have done it at some point in my life. But for all the jobs I have ever done and businesses I have had the privilege of owning, I am grateful to this day for what I learnt and the experiences they gave me. I was grateful for them at the time and I am grateful for them now.

One of the quickest ways to create a little magic in any situation is simply to tap into gratefulness, especially at work. Bringing a grateful *think magic* mindset to work can be one of the biggest game changers to your day, the work you produce and where you ultimately end up in that company. You also have no idea of the lessons you are learning that may come in very handy later on in life. When I worked on the markets, and was getting up in the freezing cold at 3 a.m., and doing a sixteen-hour day, I had no idea it would be the perfect training for the public speaking I would do later in life. Down on the markets, to stand out, you needed to shout out to the people walking past. You had to have banter, fun and tell them about the amazing bargains you had for them. This is why, no matter what public speaking I do or the size of the venue, I feel genuinely comfortable. I have done talks at the ExCeL in London to over three thousand people and even did a large seminar at the famous Hammersmith Apollo in London. That's why I'm always grateful for the opportunities I have had and why I always have a '*think magic*' mindset.

HEALTHY BUSINESS

At the health retreats we own, we point out to every team member that they don't work for us, but rather for the people who come through the doors, and of course, for themselves. I remind them that the guests arriving every week are there because they need us in some way. For some it's just a recharge and to have a little detox; for others there's much more at stake on the mental and physical health front. We may never truly know their full story, but it's up to *all* of us to create as much magic as we can for them while they're with us. Some people may have saved for a long time to come; others may have left children for the first time; some may be going through a break-up. It's different for everyone. We may not know the extent of what they are going through or why they are there, but what we do know is that we all – *as a team* – need to do whatever we can to create a healing, nurturing, inspiring, playful and loving experience for whoever walks through our doors. *Everything* matters. All the way from how guests are greeted on arrival, the cleanliness of the retreat, the quality of the freshly extracted juices, to the little extra touches all around the retreat. I believe the extra little bit of magic we try to inject into everything we do is the reason we have been full every week since the day we opened.

I remember the very first week at *Juicy Oasis* for many reasons, but the one that sticks out the most was a comment our 'hotel' manager made as people were leaving. He was used to working in massive hotel chains and as he watched the guests hugging each other, embracing our team and many crying in the most beautiful way, he said, 'You don't get that at the Marriott, do you?' It was in that moment I knew we had created something magical. I also knew that this wasn't where we *stopped* looking for ways to create magic, but rather it was the start of asking, 'How can we create *even more* magic?' We have never stopped asking this question and we never will. Nothing is ever perfect – it can't be – which is why it's only a fool who plays the perfection game. We have over forty-five different personalities coming to our *Juicy Oasis* retreat in Portugal each week, and one person's idea of magic is often different to another person's. But at least by asking the question and allowing ourselves to search for ways to add a little extra magic, we have a much better chance of creating magic for more of the guests who stay with us.

Take this book as an example. The very reason I am writing it all stemmed from asking, 'How can we create *even more* magic?' As guests arrive in their room they are greeted with a wicker basket with their name on. Everything in the basket is theirs to keep. This includes a large beach towel, a bottle of water, slippers for the spa, lavender pillow spray and a copy of our own free magazine – *Juiced!* We also have little inspirational books in the rooms for guests to read while they are there. I wanted to write my own mini book to place in the basket for guests to keep, a book that hopefully will provide them with a little added sprinkle of inspiration. You may well be at one of our retreats as you're reading this, having found your free copy in your welcome basket.

It's the same for the *Life After The Retreat* leaflet the guests are given during the Going Home talk on the last day of their stay. It was the one area of the retreat experience I felt was missing some magic. It was a very small leaflet, about ten pages, which offered some suggestions of how guests should continue after the retreat on the food and juices front. Although the retreat manager covers way more in the talk itself, the leaflet was a long way from what I would describe as magical. There are also times where people leave the retreat early due to personal reasons or can't attend the Going Home talk because they're having a treatment, so this little leaflet was all they had to go on. I felt it just wasn't us. It was OK, and we could have got away with not improving it, but we don't do 'OK' and we certainly don't do 'well, we can get away with it' either. Despite writing another book at the time, *Super Blend Me!*, I also took on the task of writing a book designed purely for the people who come to the retreats. The flimsy leaflet is now history and in its place is a wonderful 171-page, full-colour book with juice, smoothie, soup and wholefood recipes, as well as coaching and advice on what to do when you get home. It also features a 21-day challenge workbook you can go through and fill out based on the advice in the rest of the book. The point is the book guests now receive at the end of their stay, because it's been written specifically for them, has added a little more magic to the experience and, hopefully, to their future success on the health and weight front.

THE GREAT ESCAPE!

I happen to be writing this book at the location of another health retreat we're building; *Juicy Escape*. Right now, it's a forty-acre blank canvas with two large lakes in the Algarve in Portugal, and I am aiming for it to be Europe's *ultimate* health retreat. The leading question is once again, 'How can we create stupid amounts of magic?' That question allows us to become children again as we get to design the best healing, nurturing and inspirational healthy playground on earth! Just thinking about it genuinely excites me. There will be everything from amazing wooden wave pods with their own decking and a slide so you can slip straight into the lake when you wake up (I know!), all the way to an outside classic car cinema where people will be able to sit in an old classic car with no roof and watch the big screen. There'll be a gym with a boxing ring in the centre, a purpose-built spinning studio, a huge sunrise and sunset yoga platform, tennis courts, a football pitch, a games room, a spa to die for, and even little orange bikes with baskets to get around the resort. You name it, *Juicy Escape* will have it with bells on and I am beyond excited. We are even going to appoint a 'Head of Magic Making' to join our retreats team. Yes, that will be the job title! We already do what we can to create magic where possible but appointing a dedicated person whose sole job is to look for ways to create magic across all of our retreats can only raise the game further. Of all the jobs out there, I think Head of Magic Making will be a pretty exciting and uplifting career.

THE MAGIC OF SUPER JUICE ME!

We applied the same magic mentality to the ground-breaking health documentary we made – *Super Juice Me!* I wanted the film to create magic not only for the people directly involved in it, but also for everyone who watched it. If you haven't seen it, it's FREE on Amazon Prime and YouTube and here's a very quick synopsis.

We took eight people who were suffering various health conditions and put them all on the same freshly extracted juice and blend programme for twenty-eight days. The premise of the documentary was to see if you could improve, or completely alleviate, *most* lifestyle diseases by using exactly the same approach.

Instead of treating each health condition as a separate aliment or disease, I wanted the documentary to treat the individual and concentrate more on my *One Disease – One Solution* hypothesis. The results were nothing short of extraordinary and the film ended up creating magic on so many levels. It has created magic for the people who took part in the film, for the millions of people all over the world who have seen the film and it has also created incredible amounts of magic for the business and for me personally. This again is the beauty of the first rule of creating magic; you cannot create magic for others without automatically creating magic for yourself. In the same way you cannot create magic *in* your business without it also creating magic *for* your business. I found this out in spades with this documentary.

The genuine reason and driving force behind making *Super Juice Me!* was to make a difference, not to make money. The documentary cost a great deal of money to make and we made it free for all to watch immediately. We even hired the Odeon West End on Leicester Square in London for the first (and only) orange-carpet movie premiere – which again wasn't cheap! I never expected to see any of this money again as the movie was a vocation piece of work, not a business moneymaking piece of work. I was more than happy to essentially give away this money as I knew the film had the potential to make a genuine difference in this world and it was the culmination of many, many years of my work on this subject. However, even though the film was free for everyone, the money I invested in the film boomeranged back with bells on.

We filmed the documentary at *Juicy Oasis*, so when people watched the film – because the location is genuinely stunning and the results were off the scale – many wanted to come and experience it themselves. I believe one of the many reasons *Juicy Oasis* is so popular is because of the documentary. Then you had those who watched the movie but couldn't afford the retreat and therefore wanted to know the exact juice-and-blend plan used in the film, so they could follow at home and experience the same results. So I wrote the *Super Juice Me!* book and produced the *Super Juice Me!* app to make the plan open to everyone. I also have a juice delivery company and in no time at all, people who had seen the film were asking if we could supply the *Super Juice Me!* plan to save them having to make all the juices and blends at home. There is no question that the movie ended up increasing sales in every area of the company, despite the fact that it was never its intention. I have found that if your *genuine* approach to business is to make a difference first and to make money second, the law of magic will provide.

The point is the rule of magic making applies in every area of your life, including your work and business. Again, you simply cannot create magic *in* your business without you creating magic *for* your business. You cannot create magic for others without it coming back to you in more ways than you could ever imagine. The money I thought I'd be losing making the documentary has probably, inadvertently, ended up creating more than anything else I've done.

But the real magic the film has created hasn't been financial. The film has now been seen by millions of people all over the world and every week we get messages and emails expressing thanks for making it. People who have watched the film, have got inspired and taken control of their health. That's the real magic. Richard Branson's Virgin airlines even showed the film on all their aircrafts and trust me, when you're flying to the U.S. and flick through the movies and see your own film, it's a type of magic I can't even describe.

'VIRGIN' ON PURE MAGIC

Talking of Virgin, just thinking about the Virgin logo instantly brings a smile to my face. There's something about it that immediately lifts the spirits. This hasn't happened by accident. Richard Branson is, and always has been, the embodiment of creating magic in business. One of the reasons he's so successful is because he genuinely sees adventure and magic in everything he does. He gets just as excited about his company today as he did when he first started it. He looks to create magic for his customers, his team and for himself. His default is excitement, adventure and fun. One of his key tips for anyone in business is:

HAVE FUN AND THE MONEY WILL COME

And fun has always played a major part in everything Virgin has ever done. The first advert I remember for Virgin Atlantic was where you see a plane land, the steps get attached, the door opens but nobody disembarks. Then you see a balloon fly out of the door, hear party noises and the caption pops up:

'Virgin airlines, flights so good
you won't want to get off'

Genius!

I saw this advert over thirty years ago and yet I still remember that caption today. Richard wanted to shake up stuffy air travel and bring a little magic and fun to proceedings, which he did in spades. To this day he continues to create magic with Virgin and everything they do. He's not scared to step outside the norm and rock the standard business boat. I travel, a lot, and I remember the first time I went into a Virgin lounge at Heathrow airport. I walked in and honestly couldn't believe what I was seeing. If I do get to travel business class, I hardly ever use the business lounges provided by the airlines. They're usually incredibly stuffy, vanilla places with no soul. But when you walk into a Virgin lounge, it's like walking into Willy Wonka's Chocolate Factory. It just makes you smile. An airline lounge with personality, who knew?! With their cool bank of large screens, uber-relaxing and non-vanilla chairs, cute library, great food, amazing service and even a sauna and hot tub, Virgin have smashed the mould on airport lounges. But it's not just airport lounges. Virgin break out of the business mould wherever they go, always bringing fun, adventure and magic to the party.

As I write this, Virgin are building their first ever cruise ship. I've personally never been on a cruise because they've never appealed to me, but don't be surprised if you see me on Virgin's Scarlet Lady the second she's built. They just bring something different to the game and it's a simple combination of adventure, fun and magic. The Virgin brand is a mirror of its founder and magic maker, Richard Branson. It's his enthusiasm and playfulness that are channelled through every Virgin project and it's why just looking at the logo makes a lot of people smile.

I've just realised this sounds like an advert for Virgin and you'd be forgiven if you think I know Richard and I'm doing him a marketing favour. The truth is I don't know Richard and it's not an advert, but again that's the beauty of creating magic. Richard has got some random stranger, me, to big up his brand in a book. *Magic creates magic* – it's the law!

FUNNY BUSINESS

I think the person who's taken Richard's 'have fun and the money will come' mantra to a whole new level is Ricky Gervais. I appreciate comedy is subjective and Ricky Gervais might not be everyone's cup of tea but he is a whole pot of the stuff to me. Ricky is a magic maker of truly monumental proportions and the magic he's created for millions of people all over the world has boomeranged back to him on an epic scale.

We know the rule of magic making is that you cannot create it for others without it coming back in some way, but when you create magic for millions of people all over the world, expect a tsunami of magic to come flooding back to you. At the time of writing this book, Ricky has just completed the biggest stand-up comedy tour in history called *Humanity*. It was reported that he not only earned $20M from the tour itself, but also filmed one of the gigs and sold it to Netflix for a further $40M, which is pretty amazing. However, not as amazing as another magical business trick he has just pulled off. Netflix has given him another $40M for the rights to stream his next stand up tour *SuperNature*, a tour he hasn't even written yet! In magic terms, that's a pretty neat trick.

People often use the expression 'we don't want any funny business around here', but funny business is exactly the business Ricky is in. It kicked off properly for Ricky with his hit TV show, *The Office* and everything he has touched since, whether it's *Extras, Derek, Life's Too Short, An Idiot Abroad, Flanimals, Life On The Road, The Ricky Gervais Show, Animals, Politics* – the list is way too long for this little book – has literally been comedy gold for Ricky. It has also been, in a different way, comedy gold for millions of people all over the world. And what makes Ricky so successful? His desire and drive to make people laugh and be the best in the world at what he does. His desire to spread a bit of comedy magic wherever he goes in whatever he does. His genuine love for what he does and desire to make a genuine difference out there. At the end of *The Office Christmas Special*, the narrator asks David Brent, played by Ricky Gervais, 'How would you like to be remembered?' he says, 'Simply as the man who put a smile on the face of everyone he met.' I don't think this was David Brent talking, but rather Ricky himself speaking through his art.

He also uses his huge platform to create magic in another area of life he's extremely passionate about, animal welfare. Ricky is an active campaigner and does whatever he can to create magic in the animal world. The reason he's able to create magic for those without a voice is because he's managed to create magic for those with one. This is the beauty of creating magic, it has a ripple effect and you never know where the wave might end up.

THE MAGIC OF WALT DISNEY

There's magic and adventure in business and then there's the pure magic and adventure of Walt Disney. Walter Elias Disney was in the business of creating magic and even built a magical kingdom. Walt developed Micky Mouse in 1928, a character whose magic is still felt to this day by thousands of children every year. He was creative, adventurous and his mind was genuinely magical. He was the first to introduce synchronized sound and full colour three-strip Technicolor to his animation creations. He added voice to his animations and made the first feature length cartoons. He had the pure magical vision to bring to life *Snow White and the Seven Dwarfs* as early as 1937. *Pinocchio, Fantasia, Dumbo* and *Bambi* quickly followed, before he expanded his magic thinking to combine real life with animation, as seen in the magical *Mary Poppins*. In 1955, he opened Disney Land, a place built on magic. Walt Disney is one the most successful companies on the planet; it was during Walt's lifetime, and it remains that way today. Why? Because he was a magic maker of epic proportions whose business embodied the playfulness, adventure and imagination of the man himself.

THE BUSINESS OF ACTUAL MAGIC

Then you have the business of magic itself. If there was any business, or career, that is truly magical, it's magic itself. Magicians have arguably one of the best jobs in the world. They get to baffle, to dazzle and to bring instant richness and awe into someone's life. They get to literally create magic for a living. But some are more successful in the business than others. David Copperfield, Pen & Teller, David Blaine, Dynamo and the new kid on the magician block, Justin Willman, are all big players in the magic business. These magicians are said to have generated the greatest *magic money trees* of all the magicians out there. Why? Because they think big! They love what they do and always look for ways to raise the magic game. There are plenty of people out there who can do similar magic, but these people have a think-big, magic mindset that transcends that of most other magicians. They want to truly dazzle, not just with the illusion itself, but with their imagination and personalities. They want to bring their own personal extra touches and create magic in many more ways than just the trick itself.

Take Justin Willman, who does the show *Magic*

For Humans. He does similar street magic to David Blaine (the pioneer of this magical art form) and the magnificent Dynamo, but he's added his unique charm, charisma, imagination and wicked sense of humour to what he does. He is incredibly charismatic and unbelievably humble, and has brought a fresh imaginative, comedic approach to this art form and he's successful in business because of it. There didn't appear to be room for another celebrity street magician, but he has brought magic in more ways than one. This was also the same when Dynamo first came onto the scene. Street magic had been done, or so we thought. But like Justin Willman, when Dynamo popped into our lives, he brought a freshness that raised the magic game.

Unfortunately, we can't all do *actual* magic, but for businesses to be successful, creating magic must be part of the very fabric of the company. Success in business isn't all about its monetary value or what it makes financially each day. To be truly successful in business you need to have genuine love and passion for what you do, what you create and for what you bring to the table. You need to feel genuinely grateful for the opportunities that lie before you each day. The business you're in needs to excite and inspire you to *want* to get up, not *have* to get up – that's where the magic truly lies.

Do you think someone like Richard Branson *has* to get up and work ever again? He could do nothing every day for the rest of his life if he wanted; but he doesn't. The same goes for Ricky Gervais. He could retire tomorrow morning but then what? Why would he want to stop doing what he loves? Why would he stop doing the very thing that creates magic in his world? It's the same for the biggest players in the business world. Bill Gates, Warren Buffet, Tim Cook, Tony Robbins, Simon Cowell and Jeff Bezos all have enough money to never *have* to work again. The difference is, they all *want* to continue doing what they love because it's ultimately what keeps them alive. They *want* to continue to make a difference in the world.

Success is a feeling, not a number. If Richard Branson stayed in bed for days on end watching crap TV, eating junk and drinking heavily, it wouldn't matter what his bank balance was telling him, he'd still *feel* like a failure. This is because success in business is *much* more than money. To be successful in business you need to *think magic* wherever you can and do what you can to surprise, innovate, excite and make the business of *business* more enjoyable and enriching than many people think is possible.

THE MAGIC OF EMPLOYMENT

The same principle applies if you don't own the business yourself, but rather you work in one. It's just as important that you are personally invested in the business of creating magic, for others and yourself, no matter what work you do or who you work for. The average worker will spend roughly a third of their lives at work and if all you are doing is punching in and punching out with the sole goal of getting through the day, then it's only you who suffers. This doesn't mean that even with a *think magic* approach you won't have bad days at work, because that's not how it works – you clearly will, we all do – it just means your chance of having more good days goes up significantly.

COMPLACENCY CANNOT ONLY DESTROY THE MAGIC BUT YOUR BUSINESS TOO!

Whether it's my juice delivery business, the online juice academy, our health retreats or making a documentary, there isn't one part of what we do where we don't constantly look for ways to create magic. *Super Juice Me!* the movie came as a direct result of asking that question and created a magic business snowball all of its own.

Looking for ways to create magic in business, or your workplace, ultimately makes you raise your game, keeps things fresh and brings more excitement and a sense of adventure to your work and the people who experience it. A lack of creating magic, or complacency if you will, in business – whether you own it or work in it – is one of the biggest reasons businesses fail or people are 'liberated' from their position.

I cannot say this enough; if you don't want to lose your business, or your job for that matter, *think magic* and create magic wherever you can. Once again in the style of JFK:

'Ask not what the business can do for you, but what you can do for the business'

Embrace a feeling of gratitude for the opportunity you have and what you gain from it. I have seen people who clean the streets for a living but are genuinely happier than some who get paid shed-loads more in what are deemed to be better jobs. The difference is purely attitude, and finding and creating the magic in what you do.

A VERY FISHY BUSINESS TALE

The best example of 'ask not what the business can do for you, but what you can do for the business' must be that of the well-documented guys and dolls working at Pike Place Fish Market in Seattle. The fish market was bought in 1965 by John Yokoyama, who was a former employee there. In 1986, Pike Place Fish Market was on the verge of bankruptcy, but a staff meeting with a business coach changed everything. As they were searching for ways to save the business, a fish market employee suggested that they not only save the business, but also make it world famous. He talked about throwing fish, having fun with the customers, creating a show and getting the staff to enjoy their work, so the customers would too. In an interview, Yokoyama said, 'We took a stand that we were going to become world famous, we just said it and it became so.'

The truth is, they didn't just say it and it became so (that's part of the 'just ask the Universe' mantra). They *acted*! They put into practice what they discussed at the meeting and did what needed to be done, to not only save the business, but to make it world famous. Although the selling of raw, cold, smelly fish isn't exactly the most glamorous job in the world, they not only made it fun, but they gave their complete attention to each customer and made sure they had an enjoyable time buying fish. They created a 'Tom Cruise in the film *Cocktail*' type experience, but with fish! This illustrates that no matter what the business, you can add magic to it...even if it's fish selling!

For the next four years, they continued to wow the crowds and sell loads of fish, then the next level of magic hit. In 1990, the *Ted Turner Goodwill*

Games were held in Seattle. This brought with it the news crews; news crews who were quick to spot the magical atmosphere that was happening at the fish market, and they filmed them in action. In no time at all, they were on *Good Morning America*, as well as loads of other TV shows and in many magazines. Pike Place Fish Market had achieved the world-famous vision set by one of its employees in a 'what can we do to stop going bankrupt' meeting just four years earlier. Now, during the summer season, the fishmongers perform to as many as *ten thousand* daily visitors. In 1991 CNN named Pike Place Fish Market as one of the three most fun places to work in America and there are many business books based purely on the philosophy of the workers there. This piece of business magic didn't happen by accident. It happened because of a vision; a vision that was put into practice. Consistently. It happened because the employees wanted to enjoy their work more by changing, not only the way they did things, but also their attitude. It happened because they *wanted* to add fun and adventure into what they were doing – it happened because they *wanted* to create magic.

The point is, whether you own a business or work for a business, your working life becomes considerably more magical when you look for ways to create magic wherever possible. The fact is, we all end up spending a great deal of our lives working and unless we find ways to make it more exciting, rewarding, fun and magical, there's no question we'll end up being poorer for it.

I mentioned there are three main areas in life where you can create magic. We've just explored *Your Relationship With Magic* and *The Business of Creating Magic*, however, being a magic maker shouldn't solely be about creating magic for other people or for your business. Yes, it's important to create magic in these areas, but every now and then, it's also just as important to have a little...

PURE *SELF-INDULGENT* MAGIC

The Oxygen Of Life

9

I've mentioned that when you create magic for others, no matter how selfless it appears, there's always a secondary gain and you can't help but create magic for yourself in the process. I've also mentioned that although creating magic for others isn't self*less*, it's also not self*ish*. However, there is one kind of magic that appears, at times, extremely selfish and it's the kind of magic I encourage you to bathe in as often as possible – *pure self-indulgent magic*! This is where it really is all about you. This is where any thoughts of creating magic for others can take a mini vacation and where you can look for ways to create magic purely for yourself whenever and wherever you can. The beauty is the fundamental rule of magic making will still kick in and you'll find that when you tap into a little self-indulgent magic, there's *more* chance of you creating magic for others.

THE OXYGEN OF MAGIC

When you're on a plane you will hear this announcement:

'In case there is a loss in cabin pressure, yellow oxygen masks will drop from the ceiling compartment located above you. Please secure your own mask before assisting others around you.'

Or in other words, 'Sod your kids, just make sure you're OK!' Clearly that's *not* what they're saying, even though at first it does sound quite selfish. The reason they tell you to put your own oxygen mask on before helping others (including your children) is so you're in a much *better* position to be able to help them. In this situation if you help others first you'll be without any oxygen yourself. You'll get disoriented, dizzy and panicky, hardly the best state to be in to help others in an emergency.

The same principle applies to life in general. We live in an extremely fast-paced world and if you don't 'put on your own oxygen mask' every now and then, you won't be in the best state to create magic for others. At our health retreats we get a lot of people who feel guilty for either leaving their family, work or both. They feel it's selfish to have taken time away from it all, especially if there are a lot of things going on back home that need their attention. There will always be things that need our time, attention and energy but unless we find a way to create a little magic for ourselves, we'll run ourselves into the ground. It's actually extremely selfish *not* to find ways to recharge your batteries. It's selfish *not* to find ways to lift your spirits. It's selfish *not* to find moments that make *you* happy. It's selfish *not* to find ways to set aside time for a little self-indulgent magic making. If you just keep going and you're constantly pulled in a million different directions, making sure everyone else is OK and always looking for ways to create magic for others while ignoring yourself, you will have the worst of all worlds. You won't be at your best for them or for you and you'll be living in a sort of grey, non-magical limbo. You won't be living your life as your sharpest, happiest, most energetic self, which will not only have a negative effect on others around you, but also on yourself. No matter how busy your life is, you simply have to find small windows of opportunity to experience some pure self-indulgent magic. It's the oxygen of life and it's extremely hard to breathe without it. It could therefore easily be argued that by diving into some self-indulgent magic now and then, you will be in a much better position to create more magic for others.

And when it comes to creating pure self-indulgent magic, you are once again only really limited by your imagination, rather than the size of your *magic money tree*. Clearly, if you have a decent sized *magic money tree*, more options are open to you. But just like when you are creating magic for others, there are a million ways to create magic purely for yourself that require little or no money too. Self-indulgent magic can be something as simple as buying something really nice to eat, to something much bigger like booking a helicopter trip over the Grand Canyon or buying a car. It can be taking a long walk along a river, getting a massage, going for a surf at sunset, buying yourself something you've always wanted, booking a holiday, grabbing a movie, or even taking a cable car up a snow-capped mountain to enjoy the breathtaking views. Everyone's idea of personal magic will be different and everyone's access to time and money is also different, but whatever is in *your* personal grasp should be grabbed whenever possible. Self-indulgent magic doesn't always have to be something big. Most people don't realise just how easy it can be to make even the smallest, everyday things in life that little bit more magical.

BATHING IN MAGIC

Take something as simple as having a bath. You can just run it, take a quick dip and towel off; or you can create a bit of self-indulgent magic. You can light a few candles, burn some incense, put on some relaxing music, sprinkle-in some bath salts or bubble bath, pour yourself a cheeky glass of champagne and indulge in a good book or film on your tablet. The point is, you can always raise the game of any situation by asking yourself 'How can I make it more magical?' Take dinner as another example. We only get one opportunity to have an evening meal each day and you can either, not really think about it, bung something in the oven and eat it on your lap while watching TV, or you can add some magic to the proceedings – even if you're having dinner alone. Take my situation right now for example. As I write this page I am in Portugal a few miles away from a beautiful beach. I'm alone and focused on writing this book. I have a few things in the fridge for dinner, but since I have been writing this small chapter I just asked myself, 'How can I raise the magic game for dinner tonight?' Just asking the question opens up more possibilities and my dinner for tonight has totally changed on the strength of asking that question. There is an amazing sushi place on the beach, so I'll now be jumping on my little Vespa, buying some take-out sushi, and spreading a large blanket on the beach so that I can enjoy dinner watching a beautiful sunset with the waves crashing onto the shore. I have decided to raise the game even further by taking my small Bluetooth speaker so I can play a little sunset chill music at the same time. I'll take my phone and headphones so when I've finished I can make some calls and connect with people. I'll also take my swimming shorts to have a dip if the mood takes me. I genuinely had no intention of doing any of this five minutes ago, I've just decided to do it while writing this chapter. I cannot, after all, write about ways to make dinner more magical without indulging in the practice myself.

The point is, it doesn't matter where you are or what is at your personal disposal. If you are willing to search and ask the right questions, pure self-indulgent magic is yours for the taking. Yes, it may take a little more effort and thought, but the rewards are often truly magical.

PURE CARPE DIEM MAGIC

The key to a life full of moments of self-indulgent magic is the ability to tap into the magic of *carpe diem*. Carpe diem is Latin for 'seize the day' and the dictionary translation is:

> *'Used to urge someone to make the most of the present time and give little thought to the future.'*

This doesn't mean living purely in the moment with a total disregard for the future. I know people who have done that and it doesn't usually end well. No, it means in that moment give *little* thought to the future and seize the moment! It means making the most of the opportunities we have available to us. It's where we say 'f—k it!' and grab some self-indulgent magic making by the horns and run with it. It's where we seize the moment to indulge in *our* wants, *our* needs and *our* desires and where we don't let precious opportunities slip through our fingers. We will never see today ever again, so making a little time for some self-indulgent magic wherever we can is perhaps more important than we realise.

FUTURE PACE SOME MAGIC

However, tapping into the pure magic of carpe diem doesn't necessarily mean looking for a magical experience today. It's sometimes about seizing the opportunity to future pace some crazy magic for yourself. Although, as I've shown with a simple bath and dinner, there are ways to make even the smallest things that little bit more magical on a daily basis, it's quite rare for big carpe diem moments to happen on a daily basis; which is why it's important to future pace some big self-indulgent magic when you can. Organising future magic brings a certain kind of magic in itself. You get the magic and excitement of thinking about and organising it and then you get to actually experience it at a later stage. You also have the magic of anticipation, which you can draw on every day until the magical event itself.

Most people experience this when they book a holiday of some kind. Their life might be tough at the time of booking, but a certain amount of weight is lifted from their world the very second they book their magical trip. They have the excitement of thinking about where they want to go, the magic moment when they actually book it and then that wonderful magic of anticipation. When I was younger, I remember getting disproportionately excited about a holiday months before I even flew! This is because pre-planned magic has the ability to make all of the days leading up to the event a little more magical too. We all need a little light at the end of the tunnel and planning a little magic in advance is sometimes the only way to see that light.

ALWAYS MAKE SURE THERE'S A LITTLE MAGIC ON THE HORIZON

I live an extremely busy life and have many demands on my time, so I make a point of future pacing self-indulgent magic all the time. If I don't see any magic on the horizon, I make sure I create some. This can be as small as booking a massage or a concert ticket, all the way up to something as big as booking a skydive over the Great Barrier Reef, but I always make sure there's a little magic in the distance.

If you want to experience all levels of self-indulgent magic on a consistent basis, *you* have to take control and create it. It's up to you to be your own magic maker and to create the magic in your world. If you don't have any magic today, chances are it's because you didn't organise any yesterday.

Again, you can sit around waiting for the Universe to provide your magic (oh, and if you *are* sitting around waiting for the Universe, make sure you grab a book as you're in for a long wait!) or you can take control and make the magic happen. If I want the magic of seeing a 5 a.m. sunrise over the ocean, then I need to get up and make sure I'm there. If I want the magic of a full moon midnight dip in the river, again I need to make sure I turn up. If I want to experience what it's like to drive a Ferrari around Monte Carlo or see what the view is like from the top of Mount Kilimanjaro, then I just need to work out a way *I can* make it happen.

The point is, if you want more magic in your life it's ultimately up to you to create it. There are some people who, on their birthday, wait to see what magic other people have created for them, only to then get upset if the day doesn't quite live up to their expectations. If you want your birthday to be magical, *you* need to help create it. Your idea of what constitutes magic isn't necessarily someone else's so don't *hope* your individual idea of magic will just turn up, do something daily to lift *your* magic game and always make sure there's some big *personal* magic on the horizon.

MIX UP THE MAGIC

Clearly you can't create the same magic for yourself, or others, every day as it wouldn't have the same impact and would lose its magical power. I have a friend and every time I ask how he is he says, 'Outstanding!' He says this *every single time*, no matter how he's actually feeling. The theory is that by using the word 'outstanding' his brain will be tricked and no matter how he's feeling he'll always feel *outstanding*. The problem is when something gets overused it loses its power. As with drugs, the more a person has, the more tolerance they build up and the more they need to get the same result. It's the same with creating magic. You cannot simply do the same things over and over again and expect the same result. In order for the magic to keep its power, you have to be magic-smart and mix it up. Yes, you do! On that note, this is the best time to warn you that magic is easily won and easily lost so please take note: when it comes to magic making, whatever you do...

DON'T DILUTE THE MAGIC!

Use Your Magic Powers Wisely

10

As with anything in life, you can have too much of a good thing and this includes magic. For example, if I were to send my girl a beautiful bouquet of flowers completely out of the blue one day, it would probably create a little magic for her. However, if I were to send her flowers every single day, it wouldn't take long before she wasn't exactly feeling the magic anymore. In fact, far from feeling the magic, I think it's safe to say she'd soon become sick of the sight of flowers...and no doubt me! In no time at all, every time new flowers arrived at the door, instead of thinking how amazingly thoughtful I was, she'd soon be thinking how utterly unoriginal and predictable I am. If you were to cup your partner's face with both hands, stare into their eyes and tell them you love them, completely out of the blue, that moment also has the ability create pure magic. However, cup their face ten times a day, every day and tell them you love them every two seconds, don't be surprised if, instead of wanting to cup your face back, they have the desire to slap it instead! You get the point. It's extremely easy, no matter what area of your life, to *dilute the magic* and tip the balance from creating magic to creating tragic!

TOO MANY BANANAS

If you give a starving monkey a banana, they are *incredibly* grateful. However, if you give them a banana every single day from then on, the gratitude jumps to *expectancy*. If you then happen to have a surplus of bananas one month and decide to create magic by giving them two bananas every day, they once again jump to a state of gratitude. However, if you then continue to give them two bananas a day for the whole month while you have surplus, they very quickly shift from gratitude to expectancy once again. If you then go back to giving the monkey one banana, they immediately go from pure *gratitude* to *attitude*. The monkey is no longer grateful for the one banana anymore, it's now just angry with you because you haven't given it two! The monkey now *expects* two bananas a day, so when you go back to one, far from feeling incredibly grateful for the banana you are still giving it, the monkey is mad at you for removing the second banana. The monkey now feels *entitled* to two bananas a day, even though it had no bananas at all when you first met!

This scenario happens in every aspect of life, from close personal relationships to the workplace and we're all guilty of it to some extent. Therefore, it's important to be smart with your magic making and not give out '*too many bananas*' too often. If you do, not only are you in danger of diluting the magic, but of it vanishing altogether. This doesn't mean you cannot look to create magic for the same person every day, you just need to make sure you don't try to create magic by giving more of the *same* magical bananas!

A perfect example of this was when my mum offered a room to a friend of hers who had been kicked out of his home. This was a genuine '*create magic*' moment as my mum couldn't afford to have this person at the house (extra cost of utilities, food, etc.) and he was, if we're being honest, a major disruption to our lives. However, this person was in need and, as a friend, my mum wanted to create magic and put a roof over his head. Although he was working, she said he didn't have to pay anything. He said he only needed to stay for a few weeks and then he'd be out of our hair. However, many, *many* months went by and there was no sign of him making any attempt to go anywhere soon. My mum asked him if he could start paying something towards the rent and bills. Not unreasonable you'd think. The problem was, he'd had way *too many bananas*, and now *expected* to live there for free. Far from being grateful for the many, *many* months of free rent, board and generosity, he was now just completely f—ked off at having to pay anything at all. *Too many bananas*, and a jump from *gratitude* to *attitude* is easily accomplished.

You even see this at what many would describe as the most magical time of year – Christmas. If you see a kid ripping open a present and not even acknowledging it before picking up the next one and ripping that open, you've also just witnessed *too many bananas*. When you see them get mad because they didn't get the present they wanted, again you're seeing *too many bananas* in full force. Christmas is a time of *expected* magic, where most people, and especially children, are used to getting mountains of bananas. Not only do they expect this mountain, but they fully expect the bananas to be the right ones, the specific ones they wrote on a list and asked the big man with a beard for. If there's no mountain or the bananas are not of the quality they expect, all hell breaks loose. Christmas magic becomes Christmas tragic because of way *too many bananas* over the years.

This jump from gratitude to attitude only really happens in Western society. We sponsor a mixed football team – *Juice Master Utd* – at an orphanage in Cambodia, a place where they *genuinely* have nothing. Our idea of having nothing and the reality of *literally* having nothing becomes extremely apparent when you go there. We visited a small community near the orphanage where there were fifteen members of a family living in a raised bamboo hut. It was boiling hot, there were flies everywhere and their kids played on rubbish tips. These people experience the complete antithesis of a '*too many bananas*' life yet feel nothing but pure gratitude for anything they have or are given. When you see the huge beaming smiles on the faces of the children, they aren't painted on, they are as real as it gets. And if you give them anything at all, no matter how small, all you feel is gratitude in the air. You'd never, in a million years, see them throwing presents to one side and then throwing a tantrum because they're not the right presents. You'd never see them shouting at Daddy because they didn't get the pony they asked for. You only see this in some Western households at Christmas because these kids have had way, way *too many bananas* and, ironically, are all the poorer for it. There is a true richness in gratitude; it creates instant magic when you tap into it. Being able to turn on a shower and have instant, clean hot water is pure magic. It's so magical that only a couple of hundred years ago even the richest kings and queens couldn't pull this magic trick off. Having a flushing toilet, sanitation, medicine, heating, fresh food and a decent roof to sleep under are all magical. Start adding smartphones, games consoles, the internet, sight, hearing, movement, the list is infinite, and you soon realise there's a great deal of magic to feel instantly grateful for. This is why it's so sad when, at what many feel is the most magical time of the year, you see people being extremely ungrateful because they've had *too many bananas.*

Christmas should be magical. It should light up your life and it should be a time for giving. The real magic is seeing people's faces beam, or seeing them moved to tears because of the Christmas magic that's been created. I remember my mum buying me a bike one Christmas when I was kid. I had wanted a bike for a long time, but knew money was way too tight to ever believe it a possibility. On Christmas morning, I opened a small present and I remember vividly it was a cool pencil sharpener. This may seem odd, but at the time I collected unusual pencil sharpeners (don't ask, I was young!) and I was genuinely over the moon with this really unusual addition to my collection. I hugged my beautiful mum and couldn't thank her enough. Then she wheeled in a bike with ribbons on and I remember, to this day, completely losing it. I couldn't stop shaking and crying in the best possible way but also I remember telling her she couldn't afford it and we should take it back. However, there is also magic in giving and I would have denied my mum that magic if I hadn't accepted it, which she pointed out. She was also crying and I didn't understand why. It turned out she was crying because she saw I was genuinely happy with just the pencil sharpener, I think that meant more to her than my reaction to the bike.

My mum taught me gratitude above everything else. She said without gratitude you would always be poor – even if you ended up making loads of money. Gratitude is genuinely the richest feeling one can experience on a consistent basis. It nourishes the soul and focusing on what we can be grateful for can create instant magic, even on the crappiest of days. What I was most grateful for that Christmas, wasn't the pencil sharpener, or the bike (but God I loved that bike!). It was having my mum and best friend (who were one and the same person) to hang out with on Christmas Day. To think I'll never have the gift of her presence at Christmas ever again, breaks me in more ways than I can possibly describe on paper.

Like I said, I have seen *'too many bananas'* situations in all areas of life. I've seen it in business, personal relationships and over the holidays. If you own a business and you give your team an unexpected bonus one month, your team love you, but give them that same bonus every month for six months and then nothing on month seven, don't be surprised if you're no longer boss of the month! Don't be surprised if far from focusing on the extra they've had for the past six months and how amazing you are, they now hate you for not giving them the bonus. This is because they now *expect* it and you are now the bad person for taking it from them, even though in reality you haven't taken anything away at all. This is a case of *too many bananas* and why you need to be careful not to dilute the magic.

Coincidentally, I have just seen a post on social media that perfectly sums up what I am talking about here. Many years ago, I decided to run *The World's Biggest Juice Detox* where I wanted thousands of people from all over the world to join in my seven-day juice diet at the same time. I decided to make it one hundred per cent free to everyone. All people had to do was sign up and I would send them all the recipes and do daily videos to bring everyone together. I would also be on social media all week to answer their questions and keep us all focused and motivated. It was a huge success, thousands joined in from every corner of the world and I have been running a free global juice challenge four times a year ever since. The key word here is *free*. What became apparent was that although we sent the daily recipes, many felt it was much more convenient to use the app and bought it anyway. The app has way more in-depth coaching, you can auto generate your shopping list by however many days you want, it has all the recipe videos and written recipes and it means you have everything in your pocket at the touch of a button. So when we did our latest global juice challenge, we decided to make it much more convenient and even better value for everyone by making the app just 99p for a very limited time. It's better value because we apply the same 'how can we create more magic?' philosophy as we do with everything we produce, including our apps. The apps have no in-app purchases and we add crazy amounts of videos, styling and value across the board. The reason for mentioning this is because you'd think that with that added value for just 99p everyone would think 'magic!' However, although virtually everyone was extremely grateful to be able to get the app for just 99p and saw the huge added value and convenience, it seems not everyone did. Here's the tweet that literally just came in:

@juicemaster #jasonvale used to offer juice resets 2/3 times a year for free.

Excellent if you wanted to try #juicing #shame to find out you must now BUY the app to join in…

There was also a thumbs down emoji to finish the tweet. This is a perfect example of *too many bananas*! Instead of being incredibly grateful for the many years of completely free online juice challenges, this person is now mad we're charging anything at all. The craziness of it is that we made the app just 99p so that it was in everyone's reach to get the same level of help and support, and we still added support across all social media platforms and I still did bespoke videos for the challenge. All of this is irrelevant if someone has had *too many bananas*. They will never be grateful for all you have done, or look at the fairness of what you are doing. They will just focus on losing some bananas instead of seeing, if they look properly, that you added some oranges. What this person doesn't realise is that most of our apps cost an absolute fortune to produce, which puts the 99p price tag into total perspective. I also feel if someone isn't willing to invest 99p, which is less than a coffee, into a plan that can radically change their health, then I question how committed they are.

The point is, it's easy to dilute the magic if you constantly give *too many bananas*. Give your partner a candlelit massage one Saturday night, they will not only be grateful but they'll also feel the magic you've created. Give them the *same* massage every Saturday night for a few months and they soon *expect* the massage. When that happens, it won't take long before the magic gets extremely diluted. It will still feel *nice*; after all when doesn't a massage feel good after a long week? But it will feel nowhere near the same level of amazing as the first Saturday when you surprised them with it. Also, don't be surprised if the gratitude for the massage wanes somewhat and then if you miss a Saturday they might not be a happy camper – another classic case of *too many bananas*!

As I wish to hammer home, the best '*create magic*' moments come from the unexpected. That element of surprise when you do something to catch people completely off guard. The moments that often blindside someone. Moments where you can evoke a feeling of total awe and warmth in others and in yourself.

USE YOUR SIXTH SENSE TO CREATE MAGIC

Take the Movie *The Sixth Sense* for example. The magic of this film lies purely in the very unexpected nature of the ending. It totally takes you by surprise and creates that awe-inspiring magic. The point, however, is you'd never expect the same magic to happen again if you decided to watch the film for a second time. Why? Because you know the ending. You know exactly what's going to happen and what to expect. When you *expect* something, the magic isn't ever quite the same and has been diluted in some way. This doesn't mean you can't watch some movies many times over without them still creating *some* magic for you (I think I've seen *Grease* and *Dirty Dancing* about thirty times!) but in the case of *The Sixth Sense*, the magic is *all* about the surprise ending. Once you know it, even if you watched the film another thousand times, you'll never experience the same true magic of that film ever again. This is why I talk about using your 'sixth sense' when it comes to creating magic.

SMART MAGIC

Always mix up the magic so you don't totally dilute it. Keep the magic as fresh as you can and remember there always needs to be an element of surprise for big magic to be created. It's often easier to create the type of magic that truly moves a stranger than it is to move the people closest to you. Strangers don't expect anything from you at all, so by definition they'll always be blindsided and therefore, it will always be magic. When it comes to those closest to you, it's a little harder as sometimes they may have come to *expect* a little magic from you (particularly if you've written a book entitled *Create Magic*!) This is why it's extremely important to think differently and be creative with your magic. It is also vital not to overdo the magic either; it's very easy to create a '*too many bananas*' situation in any area of your life. It's also vital to be smart with your magic-making decisions. If you decide one day to give away *all* your money to create magic for someone, or see a homeless person and give him or her *your* house, you'll soon see *the* law of magic goes out of the window. Yes, magic creates magic, but if you did that, although you may feel good in the moment, your *magic* will soon feel *tragic* when you're freezing cold, hungry and sleeping in a doorway! Be smart with your magic and make sure you don't go so overboard that it strips you of any future magic-making potential.

The essence behind this *Don't Dilute The Magic* chapter is simple to grasp. Whatever magic you create for others, or even for yourself for that matter, it ceases to be *as* magical if you always do the same thing in the same way. In some cases, it stops being magical at all. You really can have too much of a good thing and it's why you need to choose your magic making wisely. There needs to be a nice balance of little sprinkles of magic to keep life ticking over, with big magic showing up every now and then. Like I say, magic is like a drug and people will soon build up an immunity to it and you'll constantly need bigger and better magic to get the same result, so space your *Big Magic* wisely, be creative and keep it as fresh as you can.

One thing is for sure when it comes to magic making, once you throw a little magic out there you're guaranteed to start...

THE RIPPLE OF MAGIC

The Snowball Effect

11

We have seen the many wonderful things that can happen when people tap into their *'create magic'* powers, not only for themselves, but also for those they are directly creating the magic for. But I feel the most magical thing that happens is the *'Ripple Of Magic'* that inevitably occurs when magic is created. There's no way of knowing where that ripple will ultimately lead or the size of the wave it will ultimately create, but if you drop a little magic pebble, expect to start a *ripple of magic*.

We saw this with Tony Robbins when the man who brought his family a basket of food one Thanksgiving ultimately led to millions of people being fed directly through the business Tony set up. It's hard to know where the ripples ultimately end and I wonder if Tony's story was the inspiration behind a Christmas Co-op advert in the UK where a young man leaves a bag of groceries at the doorstep of his housebound elderly neighbour. This Christmas advert was not only magical itself, but I'm sure inspired many people to do the same thing that Christmas. One of those people was Nigel Richardson who was so inspired by the advert that he immediately got off the sofa, grabbed his coat and drove to his local supermarket to get a bag of goodies for an elderly neighbour. It was twelve minutes past ten at night, it was cold, it was raining heavily and he said he arrived home looking like a drowned rat. He remembers the exact time because that moment was to change his life and many others. He said that '*create magic*' moment gave him such a buzz he felt reenergised and felt he had a purpose. Nigel had taken voluntary redundancy three years earlier and felt a little lost; this random act of kindness gave him purpose again. He set up Secret Hampers and has been creating magic ever since.

As I write this book, it's the British NHS's (National Health Service) 70th birthday and Nigel's first thought was 'How can we create magic for the amazing magic makers in the NHS?' He asked local businesses if they would get involved and is, as I write this, in the process of delivering seventy hampers to seventy different hospitals around the country. He wanted to create magic for the often-unsung heroes who work, day in day out making the world a better place. Although *Secret Hampers* is a business, he says it's his aim for it to become the home of random acts of kindness. He says, 'The exciting part is that the business can work on so many different levels. We're not just in the business of delivering hampers, we're in the business of creating memories, special moments and super-heroes.' When delivering a secret hamper to a care home, Nigel wanted to up the magic-making potential and added a CD with music to bring back wonderful memories for the residents. He said, 'Watching someone with dementia get up out of their chair and start dancing because of the magic we've brought – that's very special.' As was meeting a lady by the name of Ann Harvey, a resident who was lonely and at a low point in her life until she won a hamper and used it to make friends by sharing it with others. She said, 'It was the gift that kept giving', or as I like to put it, it was magic creating more magic. Nigel said one of the most special moments so far was helping a businessman surprise a team of forty doctors and nurses at a local hospital's neonatal unit that saved his premature baby boy's life.

This is *the ripple of magic* in full effect. Someone delivers a big box of Thanksgiving goodies to Tony Robbins' house; when he grows up Tony makes a vow to be successful enough to do it for someone else. Tony then creates 'The Basket Brigade', which has turned into a much bigger mission and has fed over one billion people. I am guessing, or it's one hell of a coincidence, that the Co-op's ad team were inspired by Tony Robbins and shot an advert where someone leaves a bag of food on a lonely person's doorstep at Christmas. Nigel, who was out of work, was stupidly inspired by the ad and did the same thing for a local neighbour that night. This made him feel so good he started his hamper business. He then decided to deliver hampers to doctors and nurses throughout the country as part of the NHS's seventieth birthday. I saw his tweet, as I was coming to the end of this book, and decided to add his story in. This means more people will know about *Secret Hampers* and not only will more people want to send a secret hamper to create magic, but Nigel's business will grow too. Nigel is in the business of making a difference first and making money second. When you do that and your intentions are pure, *the ripple of magic* has no choice but to also positively impact the business as a whole too. I will be contributing to the NHS70 campaign and doing what I can to add to the magic. The first thing I can do is make sure a copy of this book is added to every *Secret Hamper*. Don't you just love 'the *ripple of magic*'? It's genuinely infinite and you never truly know how many people your '*create magic*' moment ultimately touches or how far it travels.

A WORLD FULL OF MAGIC MAKERS

The wonderful truth is, the world is full of magic makers. Some sprinkle their magic in small, regular doses throughout their lives, while others create magic on such an epic scale it reaches millions of people all over the world. This may not seem the case if you always watch CNN (Constant *Negative* News) or spend your life on Twitter, but magic makers are *everywhere* and we've all, at some point or other, had magic created for us. We have all also, at times, created magic for other people and ourselves too. I believe the vast majority of us are natural born magic makers; it's in our bones, and it's within the very fabric of most people. But magic making is like any muscle and like all muscles, if you don't use it, you lose it. Well actually, the beauty of your magic-making muscle is: even if you haven't exercised it for years, it's still there waiting to be flexed.

In the film *The Wizard Of Oz*, the lion thought he had lost his courage, but he hadn't lost it at all; he just hadn't used it for a while. The same applies to magic making. The more you work a muscle, the bigger it gets. The more magic you create, the more magic you'll experience. As I said at the very start, if you want to experience more love, *create magic*. If you want to smile more, *create magic*. If you want better relationships, *create magic*. If you want a business that truly thrives, *create magic*. If you want a better working day, every day, *create magic*. If you want to feel truly alive, *create magic*. If you want to make a genuine difference in this world, *create magic*. In short, if you want to feel magic in every area of your life, all you need to do is create it. And the real beauty is, every time you use your magic-making muscle, you never know where its ripples will lead and just how much magic you may end up creating in this world.

THE ART OF MAGIC

Anyone who has ever made a movie, written a book, produced a musical, painted something beautiful, created an inspirational blog, designed a building or written a comedy, probably had no idea just how much magic their work would ultimately create. In many cases, their work creates magic for millions all over the world. Take movies for example. Movies have the ability to create magic on an epic scale. Just look at children watching the latest animation film. Their little faces light up like a lighthouse and their jaws drop in total awe of what's happening on the screen. Take the pure magic of a children's film like *Toy Story*. It was the first feature-length, computer-animated film and it paved the way for some of the most magical children's films ever made. I challenge any child, or adult for that matter, to watch *Toy Story*, *Finding Nemo*, *Shrek* or my favourite animation film of all time, *Zootropolis*, and not be dazzled by magic. As I mentioned earlier Walt Disney himself was a magic maker of epic proportions who dropped one of the biggest magic-making pebbles in history, the ripples of which are still being felt to this day. He's left a magic-making legacy that lives on and will continue to create magic for millions of children, and adults, for years to come.

The magic of film isn't confined to children of course. You've only got to look at adults watching something like the Christmas classic, *It's A Wonderful Life* to see that. Here's a movie that not only creates pure magic at the time of watching, but it's also a movie that inspires you to want to create magic for others the second the credits start rolling. I wonder how many people who didn't even watch the film, felt it's magical ripple effect? Movies move you, inspire you, and make you smile, laugh, cry and often transport you to a place of sheer wonderment and magic. I challenge anyone to watch films like *The Greatest Showman*, *Dirty Dancing*, *Miracle On 34th Street*, *Billy Elliot*, *Grease* or *Pretty Woman* and not feel pure magic jumping from the screen. I remember going to see the very first *Superman* movie when it came out at the cinema. There is no other word to describe what everyone in that movie theatre felt that evening. Magic! Movies can do that. Steven Spielberg's imagination has created more magic in film than perhaps any other producer/director in history. I challenge anyone to watch *E.T.* and not feel magic coming out of every pore at the end. Spielberg thrives on the magic he creates. He goes in disguise to movie theatres where they're showing his new movies to feel the atmosphere and to experience the magic he has created. Creating magic in film is his oxygen, it's what makes him tick and it's the very thing, along with his family, that ultimately keeps him alive. He's a natural born magic maker who has taken consistent action to create magic for as many people as possible. By doing so, because of the law of magic making, he has created magic for himself beyond most people's wildest imagination. Richard Curtis is another writer/producer whose movies and sitcoms have magic at their core. But Richard's magic-making ripples reach much further than those created by *Love Actually*; *Bridget Jones Diary*; *Notting Hill*; *Four Weddings And A Funeral* and comedy masterpieces like *Blackadder.* He, along with another of life's magic makers, Lenny Henry, created *Comic Relief*, an incredible charity that has raised millions of pounds of magic-making money for the neediest people in the world. Richard and Lenny have used the ripple created by their fame in the arts to create a wave of true life giving magic for millions in need.

Books are another wonderful example of magic making. Like films, books have the ability to transport you to magical places. Take *Harry*

Potter, a book with magic at its core. It's a book that's transported millions of young children, and adults alike, into a unique magical world. When J. K. Rowling sat down and put pen to paper I bet she never imagined in her wildest dreams the amount of magic she would end up creating for so many. Make no mistake, the *Harry Potter* series has also created a lot of magic for J. K. herself, not just in knowing her work has brought awe and wonder to so many children, but her *magic money tree* is in full bloom because of it. That can be one of the many magical side effects when you create magic for others on that sort of scale. Children's books in general are all about creating magic and one of the original magic makers in children's literature is the one and only Roald Dahl. The story of *Charlie And The Chocolate Factory* is still to this day, one of the most imaginative and magical stories ever written. It created magic for the first child who ever read it and it continues, along with his library of other amazing magic-making books, to lift the spirits of thousands of children, and adults, every single day. That's the beautiful ripple effect of creating magic. Today, it's people like David Walliams, Tom Fletcher and Alesha Dixon who are bringing their unique playful magic-making imaginations to the children's book arena. Books that will continue to create magic for children for many years to come. They all have magic in their minds, and their books transport children to places only their playful imaginations could take them to.

Then you have a book like *Fifty Shades Of Grey,* which created a very different kind of magic for millions of people. I am sure that when E. L. James first put pen to paper, she had no idea just what a ripple, and in many cases shudder, it would create. She created a tsunami of magic and has experienced one in return. The *ripple of magic* from the *Fifty Shades Of Grey* series is still being felt today. It broadened many people's sexual horizons and no doubt raised the magic stakes in bedrooms all over the world.

Of all the art forms, perhaps the one that has the power to create the most amount of magic is music. Music can move you, inspire you, lift you and has the unique ability to transport you to truly magical places simply by closing your eyes. Elvis Presley, The Beatles, The Stones, The Jacksons, David Bowie, Aretha Franklin, Prince, Pavarotti, Ed Sheeran plus thousands of others, have all created magical ripples that will be felt for generations to come. One man who has beautifully combined this magical art form with a relatively new art form is the truly magical James Corden. His *Carpool Karaoke* on YouTube has brought a new kind of musical and visual magic to hundreds of millions of people. I like all of them but the most magical for me has to be the one with Paul McCartney, which takes you on a glorious twenty-three-minute magical ride.

Then you have art. Look at something as magical as the Sistine Chapel ceiling. Michelangelo painted this magnificent piece of art between 1508 and 1512 and this stunning piece lives on to create magic for hundreds of thousands of people every year. There are way too many examples of paintings and sculptures to add to this small book, but each piece carries its own magic. Sometimes that magic will be individual and create magic for a few. And other times, like in the case of the Sistine Chapel, it will provide magic for millions.

But whether it's music, film, literature, architecture, ballet, opera, painting, sculptures, dance, magic itself or any other art form, we all get to experience their magic. That magic is different for everyone – especially in the arts – one person's magic is perhaps another person's idea of tragic, but there is such a huge variety in every art form that we always find something magical to *us*. Millions of movies have already been made, millions of books have already been written, millions of paintings have already been painted, millions of sculptures have already been crafted, millions of iconic buildings have already been built and millions of truly magical moving pieces of music have already been recorded. We live in such a beautifully unique time where we get to bathe in the magic others have already created. Again, everyone's idea of magic is different, but whether we realise it or not, we all have our own personal magic makers that lift our world and create more magic for us than perhaps they'll ever know.

For example, I am unsure if the entertainers, business people and musicians I have mentioned in this book, as well as, of course, the writers and actors of the greatest comedy series of all time, F.R.I.E.N.D.S, will ever know the amount of magic they have created throughout *my* life and the ripple effect it has had. We all have our own personal lists and no doubt many on my list won't be on yours, but we all have a list of magic makers who have brought a great deal of magic to *our* worlds. Magic makers who often have no clue of the sheer volume of magic they create and what a difference they truly make in this world.

Ricky Gervais will never know how many times he's had me doubled over with laughter and James Corden will never know how many times he's made me smile and made my day that little bit better. Robbie Williams will never know how many times he's entertained me beyond belief and David Beckham will never know how many times his right foot has made me leap out of my chair. Ed Sheeran and James Morrison will never know how many times they've transported me to a completely different world. Steven Spielberg and Richard Curtis will never know how many times they've made me look up at a screen in awe or how many times they've made me laugh or moved me to tears. And Tony Robbins will have no idea how he completely transformed my life and ultimately created more magic than I could ever have imagined. If it wasn't for Tony's words of inspiration on a course I listened to *many* years ago, I probably wouldn't have ever have had the confidence to write my first book. If I hadn't written the first book, I wouldn't have written the second, third, fourth or fifteenth. If I hadn't written that first book I would never have made my movie, opened my retreats, made the apps, produced my magazine or even be writing this book now. If I hadn't written that first book then I wouldn't have received this email that has literally just this second, as if by some kind of serendipitous magic, landed in my inbox as I write these very words. I think it's the perfect place to share it with you:

....

"Our father is in his 60s. Fourteen years ago we lost our mum, his wife, to breast cancer and since then he's lived on convenience foods. Just over four years ago I was diagnosed with cancer at 34 and I decided to start juicing.

Last year he developed acute psoriasis and after light therapy made it worse, his dermatologist offered him a chemotherapy drug. She told him creams wouldn't do anything and that it was an inside out job. That's when he had the breakthrough moment! He called me and said I want to talk to you about juicing, as I don't want to start a chemo drug when I don't have cancer! Within a matter of weeks he started your 28-day juicing plan and lost over 42lbs, his skin has cleared up too!

I wondered if you could drop him a letter to congratulate him on his success? The Dad we had before my mum died is back. I cannot begin to describe to you the transformation, physically, mentally and emotionally. Thank you for bringing our dad back! I really mean that. To lose one parent was gut wrenching, but when you see another suffer it's heart breaking. You've changed that.

Huge love and keep juicing.”

....

I will of course send him a nice card and raise the magic bar for him in some way too. It's hard to describe what emails like that mean to me or just how much they move me. I suffered with psoriasis from head to toe and was also told there was nothing that could be done. To hear of this man's incredible change and renewed love for life because of something I have written, creates more magic than any lottery win ever could. When I wrote my first book, I simply said, 'If it helps one person, then it's worth writing.' But millions of people have now read my juicing, health and addiction books, millions have now seen my movie; and I've received thousands of letters from people all over all over the world whose lives have changed for the better. But we need to always remember *the Joey Rule* – that there's no such thing as a selfless good deed – because this personally brings me more magic than you can ever imagine.

The main point is that the little ripple of magical confidence Tony Robbins created for me as I listened to him led to me having the courage to write my first book, which in turn created more ripples, and has helped to create a little magic for thousands all over the world – including this man. This is *the ripple of magic* in full effect and it illustrates how one piece of magic making inevitably leads to another and another and another.

You will never know how many ripples your magic will create or how far they will reach, but know that when you create magic, you will have started a ripple.

Just think how many people have felt the positive ripples of magical change created by the huge magic makers of the world. People like Martin Luther King Jr, Emmeline Pankhurst, Nelson Mandela, Rosa Parks and Mahatma Gandhi. We all feel the ripples of magic created by people who we'll probably never meet, people who have made a profound difference in our lives and who help us to live in a more magical place.

However, the biggest magic makers in your life will usually be those who are, or come, close to you. It's your friends, your family and, at times, just people who come into your immediate world, even if only fleetingly, and make your life just a little more magical. That's the true beauty of magic, it can hit you at any time, anywhere, come from anyone and sometimes in the most unexpected ways.

A PERFECT *KNIGHT* FOR A LITTLE MAGIC

Many years ago, at the last retreat we ever hosted at a place we hired, which happened to be a private island, we had the honour of having the extraordinary soul singer Beverley Knight attend the retreat. At the end of the week, and completely out of the blue, Beverley stood up as we were all finishing our end-of-retreat dinner and tapped her glass to get everyone's attention. She then started to sing, completely acapella, silencing and captivating everyone with three of her tracks. The expression 'goosebumps' is often overused, but there's no better word to describe what her singing created for everyone. Beverley also changed the words of her track *Gold* and added in my name so I had a personal rendition. This is what I talk about when I say magic can hit you anytime, anywhere, by anyone and sometimes in the most unexpected ways. This was *completely* unexpected. Beverley created breathtaking magic at the end of what was a very magical week, not just for me, but for all the people who were there and no doubt for herself too.

TAKE THAT FOR A BIT OF MAGIC

Gary Barlow did the same when he came to the retreat a few years later. He didn't sing at the end like Beverley, but he created some very personal magic for me. When I first started running my retreats, I always used to finish the final rebounding session of the week with *Never Forget* by Take That. When I was growing up I was a *huge* Take That fan (don't judge!) but after Robbie Williams left, the band separated and Take That were no more. When we all bounced to *Never Forget*, I used to joke how important it was to pay homage to the boys and put some energy out there to get them back together. Then after ten years away, Take That – minus Robbie – decided to reform and do a comeback tour. Their tour manager, Linda, came to our retreat and saw I was paying homage to the boys and said she'd get me tickets for the comeback tour. I had no idea at that stage Gary would ever come to the retreat personally, so you can only imagine how blown away I was when he did. He booked the whole place and there was just him, his crew and the odd *Spice Girl* thrown in for added magical measure. Although I wanted the weather to be amazing for his stay, it turned out to be the most awful weather week *Juicy Oasis* had ever seen. However, spirits weren't dampened and it turned out to be a pretty amazing week to say the least.

What made it truly unforgettable for me personally was the bit of magic Gary created at the end of the week. Gary hadn't been to any of the mini trampoline sessions all week – yoga is way more his thing – and the final rebounding session of the week was no exception. Gary was in the sauna as we all bounced our way to finishing the week in style. As it was the final rebounding session of the week and as I was giving the class, I did what I always do and played *Never*

Forget. About half way through as I turned to face the river, hands in the air, bellowing out the track, I heard 'Hello Jason!' It was Gary Barlow on a mini trampoline behind me joining in with *Never Forget*. He had got out of his warm sauna, put on some gym gear and came over purely to create some magic for me. It was an amazing gesture and I am sure, even to this day, he has no idea of the level of magic it created. I had been bouncing to *Never Forget* at the final rebounding session of the week at the retreats for many years and suddenly, there was Gary himself joining in. At the end of the week, Gary said it had been one of the best weeks of his life and asked if he could thank us by playing at the launch of *Juicy Escape*, for free – *could it be magic*? (little ref to a Take That track there, for those who don't know!)

Beverley Knight didn't have to sing at the end of her week and Gary didn't have to come and bounce on a mini trampoline to *Never Forget* at the end of his week or offer to sing at the opening of my next retreat. They do things like this because creating magic is their default and it's the very reason why they are as successful as they are.

THE DEEPEST MAGIC OF ALL

As magical as the moments are where we're completely taken aback by people we don't really know, who come into our lives and sprinkle their magic; the deepest magic usually comes from those who are very close to us. My mum, as I have said many times throughout this book, was without question my biggest ever magic maker. She couldn't write, sing, act or give a personal development seminar, but she was my most prolific magic maker. Her magic came through her caring, her laughter and her pure unquestionable and unconditional love. The beauty, though, of the *ripple of magic* is that my mum's wonderful '*create magic*' mindset didn't end when she passed away. Her magic-making influence is in my blood, it's in my DNA and, through me, I'm hoping her magic making will live on in some way. I am also hoping I can pass the magic-making genes onto my son, little JJ, who came into this world at the same time I started writing this book. He, in turn, I hope will pass it down the generations so that my mum's natural '*create magic*' gene will live on forever.

WE'RE ALL MAGIC MAKERS

No matter what is happening in your life or where life has taken you, we *all* have the ability to create more magic than we realise and we already create more magic than we know. We also have more magic created for us than we realise too. Those closest to us often have no idea just how much magic they bring to our world, but equally we often have no idea of the level of magic we bring to theirs either. I'm not sure if my Katie knows just how much magic she creates in my life on a daily basis and I've no idea how much I bring to hers. Little JJ has no idea how much magic he brings with just a smile and a giggle and I'm sure at this stage he doesn't appreciate the magic we bring to him. I'm sure my beautiful god-daughter, Robyn, doesn't have a clue how much magic she's brought into my world since the day she was born and I am also sure I don't know the magic I perhaps have brought to her world either. The same goes for my amazing nephew Alfie, my gorgeous niece Molly, my wonderful friends and the incredible team in my juicy business. All of them probably have no idea of the level of magic they create in my world and I have no idea of the amount of magic I help to create in theirs. The point is, there's magic all around us and to experience it, all we have to do is create it – yes, it really is that simple.

GO FORTH AND CREATE MAGIC

Create magic in your work, in your business, in your relationships, for strangers and create magic for you, *consistently* – it's the oxygen of life that will enhance every aspect of it. Life is simply a ninety-year journey; the first five years we're dribbling and the last five years we're dribbling.

But what makes it all worthwhile are the magical adventures in-between. Magic we get to experience, magic we are in control of and magic, above all, *we* have the power to create. And that's the main point here. *You* have to go out and create the magic; *you* have to make it happen – magic making is in *your* hands. If you simply sit on your derrière asking the Universe to create some magic for you, don't be surprised if all the magic in every area of your life does a disappearing act.

If I want to experience the magic of interviewing some of my magic-making idols I mentioned in this book for my *Create Magic Podcast* series, like Tony Robbins, Richard Branson, Ricky Gervais, James Corden, David Beckham, Robbie Williams, Richard Curtis, David Walliams, Tom Fletcher, or any of the others, I can't just ask the Universe – I need to actively *do* something in order to try and create that magic. You can't just *hope* magic will happen, you have to make it happen. Gary Barlow didn't just turn up at my retreat one day because the Universe sent him. He came because after running retreats for over fifteen years, word got out and someone who knew him came, loved it so much, and encouraged him to come. But to be in the position of meeting Gary Barlow and experience the magic, I needed to have written fifteen books, made a movie and built a retreat first!

BUILD YOUR MAGIC MUSCLE

The key is to start to build your magic-making muscle. You need to make creating magic as automatic as brushing your teeth. It needs to become your default, the thing your subconscious brain naturally leans towards. For some people that's already the case; they're born magic makers and it comes naturally to them. Doctors, nurses, fire fighters, foster parents, humanitarians and teachers are all amazing examples of natural born magic makers who make a huge difference every single day to so many. They're the bedrock of create magic and genuine heroes. However, for others magic making might be brand new, so you may need to pop into the magic-making gym and start building that muscle. You can start small, but you'll find the more you work your muscle, the more opportunities open up to you. You can start small, but you'll find the more you work your '*create magic*' muscle, the bigger the magic-making opportunities open up to you. You'll find you'll have more power to create bigger magic for others, which in turn, will give you the opportunity to create bigger magic for yourself. This is why at the back of this book I have added a small, but potentially powerful, *Create Magic Workbook*. I have added this for one reason and one reason only, so you don't leave this book without immediately doing something to flex your magic-making muscle. You should never lose sight of a goal without doing something towards that goal, *immediately*. If your goal is to create magic in every area of your life, then tap straight into your magic-making potential by doing the mini workbook at the back of this book.

Funnily enough, Richard Branson, as if by another bit of serendipitous magic, has just posted this on his twitter profile as I write this very page:

'Picture yourself when you're 90 years old,
sitting in a comfortable chair, asking yourself:

WHAT HAVE I DONE IN MY LIFE?

We should all aim to look back at life with no
what-ifs, and be proud of what we've achieved.'

And nothing will make you prouder or enable you to achieve more in your life than joining the magic-making army. That is the aim of this book, to create an army, or family if you will, of magic makers all over the world who create magic for others. My aim is to show we all have the power to create magic, regardless of how big our *magic money tree* is, or where we are in life at this moment. My aim is also to show you there are a million ways to create magic and that it's often the smallest things that can create the biggest amounts of magic. Ultimately though, the aim of this book is to help create stupid amounts of magic, through *the ripple of magic* effect, for millions of people all over the world. That's why I encourage everyone to hand a copy of this book to everyone they know. Give a copy to all in your company, to your friends, your partner and to anyone you want add a little magic to. I want this book to create magic in itself and I want it out there in the world doing what it was born to do.

However, just before you go forth into the world to create magic, I have one last thing to show you. Throughout the book I have said there is no such thing as a selfless good deed (*the Joey Rule*) but there's always an exception to every rule. This is a something that was brought to my attention by a friend only a week ago, and I cannot think of a more magical way to end the book. Get your tissues at the ready as we discover...

THE EXCEPTION TO THE MAGIC RULE

"Today, I operated on a little girl. She urgently needed type-O blood, but we didn't have any. Thankfully her twin brother had O blood. I explained to him that it was a matter of life and death. He sat quietly for a moment, and then said goodbye to his parents. I didn't think anything of it until after we started to take his blood and he asked, 'So when will I die?' He thought he was giving his life for hers! Thankfully, they'll both be fine!"

Dr. Jim Clark

YOUR *CREATE MAGIC* MINI *WORKBOOK*

THE MAGIC OF TAKING INSTANT ACTION!

Welcome to the mini, but potentially powerful, *Create Magic Workbook*. Think of this as your induction into the *'create magic'* gym where you get to make an immediate start on building those magic-making muscles. This is where you get the chance to make some instant magic-making decisions in the key areas of your life:

★ **RELATIONSHIPS**

★ **WORK / BUSINESS**

★ **STRANGERS**

★ **YOURSELF**

You will see that in each section of this mini workbook, I have left room for three ideas for each of these key areas. The idea of course is not to simply write down how you can create magic in these areas, but to put those ideas into *immediate* action.

There are many people who talk about doing things or wish for things to happen, instead of taking action to make sure they happen. Hopefully, after reading this book you should feel inspired to create magic in every area of your life. Just the thought of it should feel exciting. What you need to understand is that the momentum created by this book, like all momentum, can slowly fade. This is why, if you're serious about joining the magic-making family and serious about changing your life through the power of creating magic, you need to start implementing it now. You need to take immediate magic-making action so you start to build that muscle straight away. You don't want to lose this momentum. If you think you don't need to worry if momentum is lost because you can simply read the book again, remember the *Sixth Sense* philosophy – the book can never be *exactly* the same again. The best time to harness its magic momentum is now. With that in mind, let's put this into practice and start to…

BUILD YOUR MAGIC MUSCLE

ALL MAGIC BEGINS WITH A SIMPLE QUESTION

At the very start of this book I said if you want more magic in any area of your life, all you have to do is create it. I also mentioned that all magic making starts with a question. I pointed out that the question, although deceptively simplistic, has the potential to have a bigger positive impact on your life and the lives of others than any other question you can consistently ask yourself. And that *Magic Question* is of course:

'HOW CAN I CREATE MAGIC...?'

How can I create magic... *in my relationship?*

How can I create magic... *in my work/business?*

How can I create magic... *for strangers?*

How can I create magic... *for myself?*

You can finish the 'How can I create magic...?' question any way you like, but your brain will only come up with ways to create magic if you ask it to. This is why this mini workbook is made up of only four simple but powerful questions. Four questions that cover all the major areas of your life where creating magic will have the biggest impact.

I have left room for three answers to each of these questions – three ideas of how you can create magic in each of those key areas. When you ask each question, ask them with conviction. And when you ask them, always allow space for your creative brain to come up with some cool and exciting answers. Remember, sometimes it's the smallest things that create the biggest moments of magic, so be creative.

I hope you get a chance to listen to the *Create Magic Podcast* series and I look forward to seeing your magical stories on the *Create Magic Instagram* account (@createmagicofficial).

In case our paths never cross, I'd like to thank you for joining the magic-making family, for all the magic you'll ultimately create, and I wish you a life full of pure magic!

Love Jason ★

HOW CAN I CREATE *INSTANT* MAGIC IN MY RELATIONSHIPS?

1. ....

....

....

....

2. ....

....

....

....

3. ....

....

....

....